Keyboarding and
Document Presentation

Related titles in the series

Accounting
Advertising
Auditing
Book-keeping
Business Law
Business Studies
Business French
Business German
Business Italian
Business Spanish
Commerce
Cost and Management
    Accounting
Economics

Elements of Banking
Financial Management
Human Resource Management
Information Technology
Law
Management Theory and
    Practice
Marketing
Office Procedures
Psychiatry
Social Services
Statistics for Business
Teeline Shortland

Keyboarding and Document Presentation

Second edition

Ruth Waxman
Business Studies Lecturer

Lyn Woods
Business Studies Lecturer

MADE SIMPLE
B O O K S

Made Simple Books
An imprint of Butterworth-Heinemann Ltd
Linacre House, Jordan Hill, Oxford OX2 8DP

ℛ A member of the Reed Elsevier plc group

OXFORD   LONDON   BOSTON
NEW DELHI   SINGAPORE   SYDNEY
TOKYO   TORONTO   WELLINGTON

First published 1992
Reprinted 1992, 1994
Second edition 1996

© Butterworth-Heinemann Ltd 1992, 1996

British Library Cataloguing in Publication Data
Waxman, Ruth
  Keyboarding and Document Presentation –
  2Rev.ed
  I. Title   II. Woods, Lyn
  652.3024

ISBN 0 7506 2550 3

Printed and bound in Great Britain by
Martins the Printers Ltd, Berwick upon Tweed

Contents

Preface

In today's business and learning environment almost everyone will be faced with the need to use a keyboard with some degree of competence. This book has been written to enable students to attain a level of proficiency in keyboarding skills that will allow them to cope with the demands of the electronic age.

Although written primarily for students preparing to take RSA Stage I and II or Pitman/LCC Elementary II examinations and GCSE, it is equally suitable for those wishing to acquire essential skills for use on a Typewriter, Word Processor or Computer keyboard. Included is a Personal Competency Checklist which is ideal for students aiming for GNVQ/NVQ accreditation.

In this book we have used the **vertical method** (see explanation) of learning the keyboard. Teaching in both Schools and Colleges of Further Education, we have found this method has proved to be the most successful and enjoyable for students as they quickly achieve accuracy and speed. Their interest is maintained as they are continually motivated by their achievements and as a result are less likely to give up. Other methods require students to spend a great deal of time typing sequences of odd letters. The **vertical method** enables the student to type short sentences from the start.

In compiling this book, we have used, to the best of our knowledge, entirely fictitious names for people, places and companies.

Ruth Waxman, Cert Ed, TDipWP
Lyn Woods

How to use this book

Prior to starting, it is important to read through the explanation of the **vertical method** and the sections headed **Before you start** and **Preparing to type**.

The book is divided into five chapters for easy use, and at the back, a fold-out 'hand' diagram is provided which can be filled in as new keys are learnt.

Where appropriate, icons will appear in the margin to mark which instructions are specifically for typewriter users and which are for wordprocessor users .

Chapter 1   Learning the Keyboard (sub-divided into 6 units)

The student is advised to work through the individual units in steady stages, moving on to the next one only when fully confident with the keys.

It is important at this stage not to rush the work, as this will lead to inaccuracy and lack of confidence.

Before starting a new unit, it is a good idea to go back over some of the previous work in order to 'warm up'.

Chapter 2   Fundamental Keyboarding Skills

By working conscientiously through this chapter the student will become competent in all aspects of keyboarding. These are fully explained and backed up with examples.

Students will also become more familiar with the facilities available on their machine.

Chapter 3   Document presentation

Having acquired the necessary skills in Chapter 2, Chapter 3 goes on to apply them.

Letters, memoranda, display, tabulation, forms etc. are all fully explained with detailed examples and the student is provided with numerous practice exercises to test and stretch his/her knowledge.

In order to obtain the maximum benefit from this chapter we suggest that when the student feels confident with a topic, he/she moves on to next one. The work can then be varied by selecting different exercises within this chapter.

Chapter 4   General Keyboarding Information

This section is devised to be used as a constant source of reference. Students will find it invaluable when working through the practice exercises.

A Personal Competency Checklist is also provided for the student to 'tick off' the skills fully acquired; this is a useful guide to knowledge gained.

Chapter 5   Assignments

Each assignment consists of 5 related tasks which make use of all the skills learnt. They are designed to simulate actual situations and the student should set aside enough time (approximately 1 to 2 hours) in order to work through and complete a whole assignment in one session.

They are also excellent preparation for any of the Examination Boards.

The vertical method

Whichever method is used to learn the keyboard the middle line known as the **home keys**, have to be learnt initially, as they are the 'base' for the fingers at all times.

The **vertical method** uses the system whereby individual vertical rows of keys are identified, line by line, thus building up a pattern which is easily remembered.

The index and middle finger on each hand begin the 'pattern' by coming from the top row of letters, on to the home key line and eventually down to the bottom line. As the sequence becomes familiar, additional letters on adjacent vertical lines are introduced until the whole keyboard has been covered. Whilst the new letters are being introduced, those previously learnt are continually being revised, thus ensuring a thorough knowledge of the keyboard.

QWERTY KEYBOARD
LAYOUT

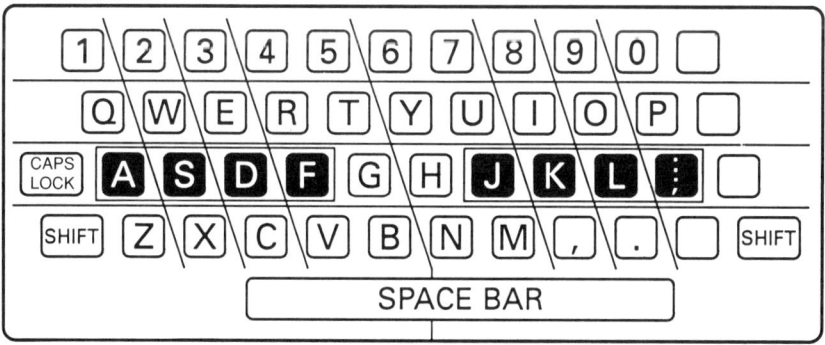

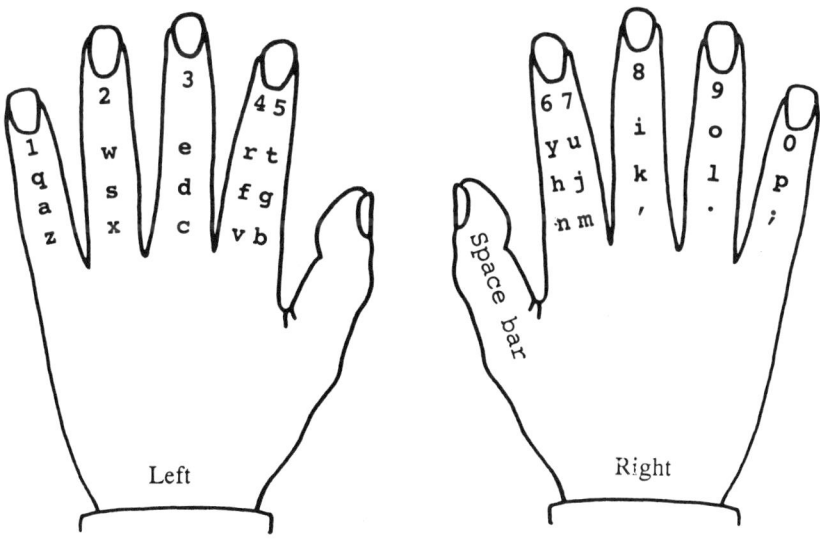

Left   Right

Before you start

As you will be spending some time at the keyboard, in order to prevent aches and tiredness, ensure that you are sitting correctly in a chair which can be adjusted to suit your height and which will support your back. Your feet should be flat on the floor for balance and you should be a comfortable distance from the keyboard - do not 'hunch' over the machine.

Make sure that the lighting and ventilation are good, and that the book you are working from is suitably placed for easy use, thus avoiding any possibility of eye strain. Taking regular breaks away from the keyboard will also help you avoid eye strain.

Hand position is also very important for efficient keying in. The fingers should be curved and hovering over the home keys, thumbs over the space bar. Do not allow your wrists to 'sag' and rest on the keyboard as this restricts your movement and could lead to serious hand problems.

Adequate lighting/ ventilation

Back well supported in suitable chair

Comfortable work station

Fingers over 'home keys' wrists not sagging

Feet flat on floor

Preparing to type

 Insert your paper into the machine, taking care that the edge of the paper lines up with the 0 on the left-hand side and that the paper is straight.

Set your **line spacer** to **single line spacing**. Position the **left-hand margin** at 12 and the **right-hand margin** at 72. If using an electronic machine, refer to the manual for margin setting.

Type the keys as they are dictated. Do not rush. If working alone, say each letter aloud as you type it. This will enable you to have a good typing rhythm, and by saying the letter aloud you will find that you remember the positions of the keys more easily.

When you need to leave a space between the letters/words, tap the **space bar** with the thumb of your right hand.

After you have typed each group, return the carriage **twice** before starting the next group. This is known as 'double line spacing' and is the spacing required between each new paragraph.

Chapter 1
Learning the Keyboard

UNIT 1 Home keys: a s d f   ; l k j

Overview

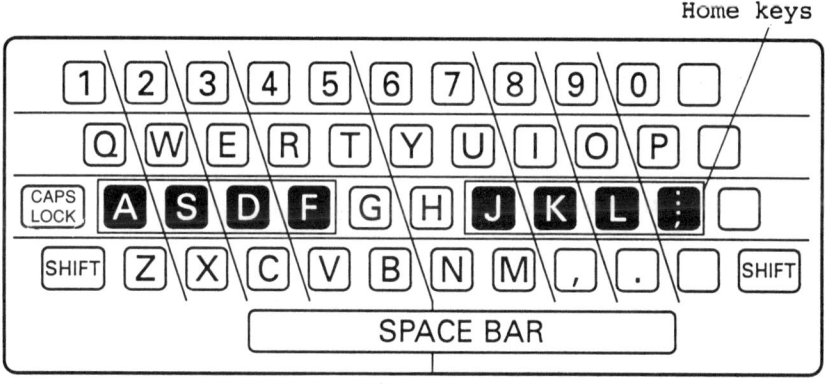

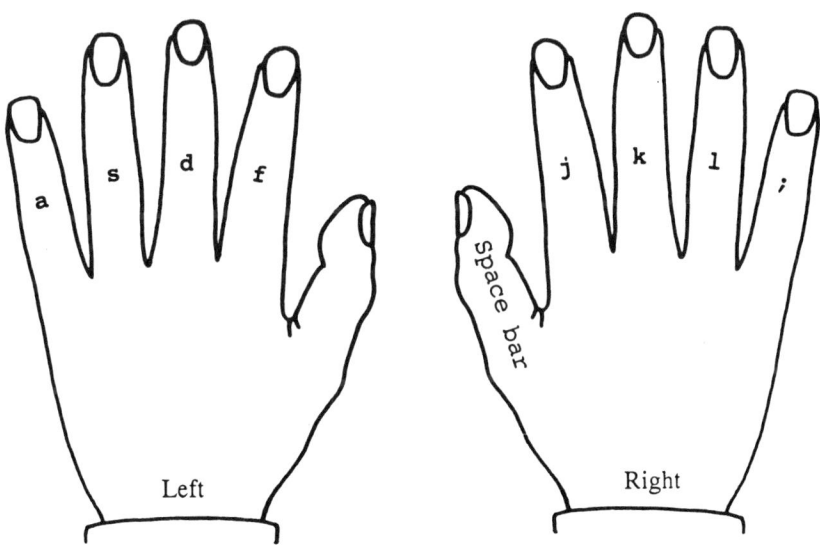

Left

Right

UNIT 1   Home keys: a s d f   ; l k j

The row of keys in the centre of the keyboard are known as **home keys**. They are called **home keys** as your fingers rest or hover over them at all times, only moving from them to use other keys.

The home keys are: a s d f   ; l k j

Home keys

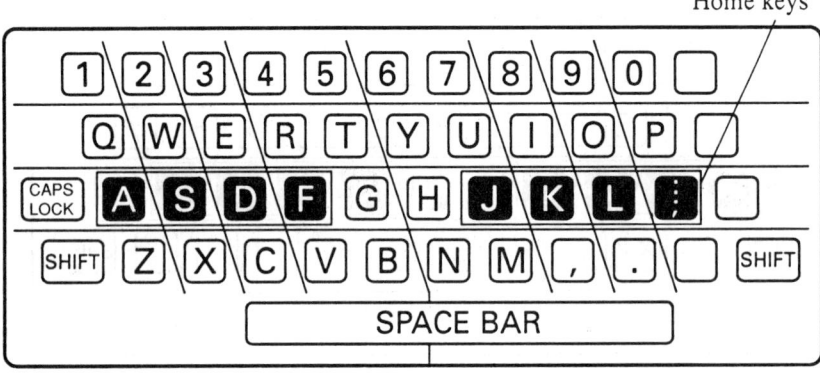

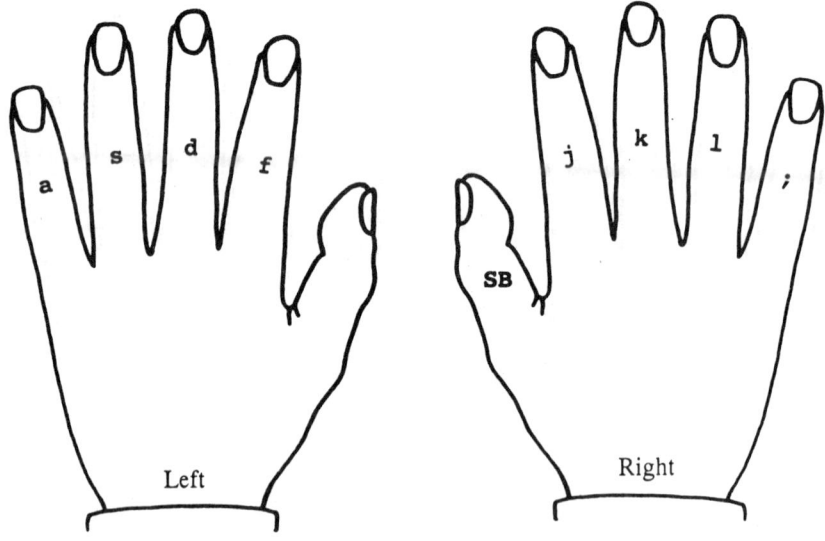

Write them on the 'blank hands' diagram provided at the back of the book.

Place your fingers on the **home keys** as instructed.

NOW YOU ARE READY TO BEGIN TO TYPE.

GROUP A

```
asdf ;lkj asdf ;lkj asdf ;lkj asdf ;lkj asdf ;lkj asdf ;lkj
asdf ;lkj asdf ;lkj asdf ;lkj asdf ;lkj asdf ;lkj asdf ;lkj
```

GROUP B

```
jkl; fdsa jkl; fdsa jkl; fdsa jkl; fdsa jkl; fdsa jkl; fdsa
jkl; fdsa jkl; fdsa jkl; fdsa jkl; fdsa jkl; fdsa jkl; fdsa
```

Repeat the above groups at least 5 times.

Try these simple words. Copy each group at least 5 times.

```
sad dad fad adds sad dad fad adds
lad; jaffa; salad; fall; lass; jaks;

dad adds jaffa salad; dad adds jaffa salad;
lass; sad lad falls; lass; sad lad falls;
```

UNIT 2 New keys: e r t g   h y u i   numbers: 3 4 5   6 7 8
Overview

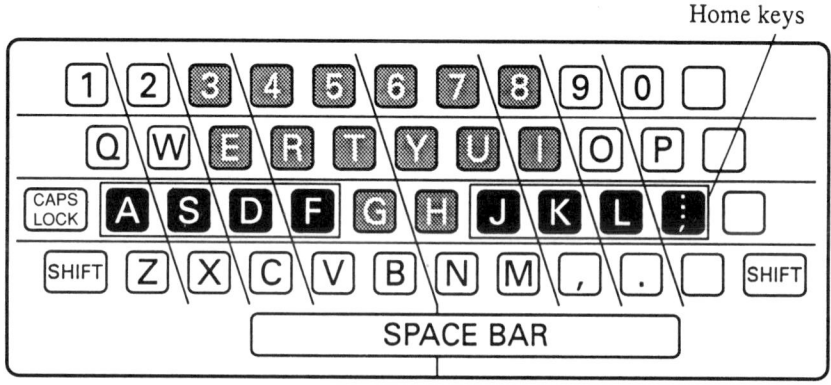

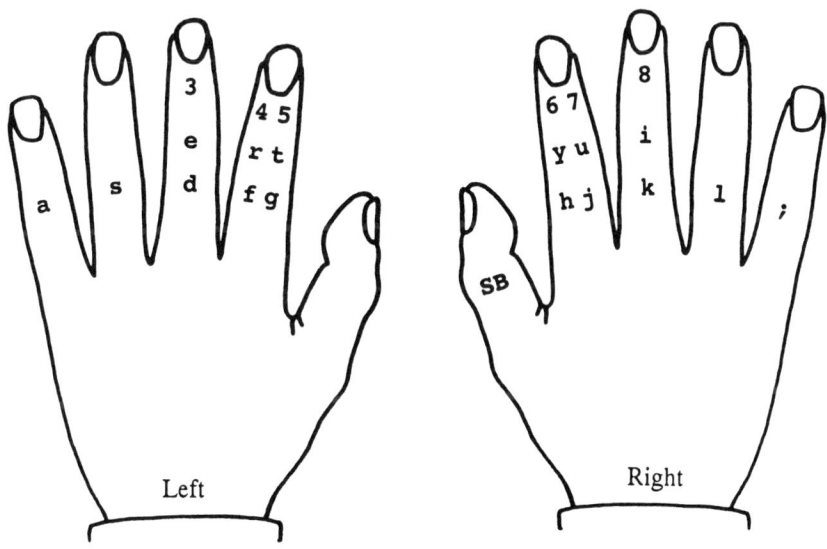

UNIT 2 New keys: e r t g h y u i

Add these to the diagram provided.

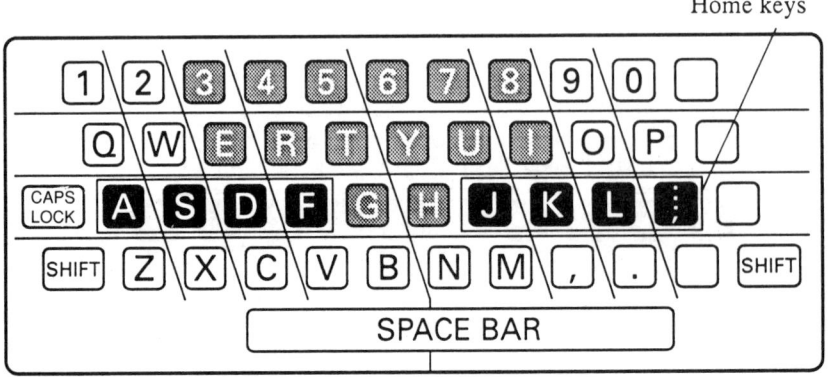

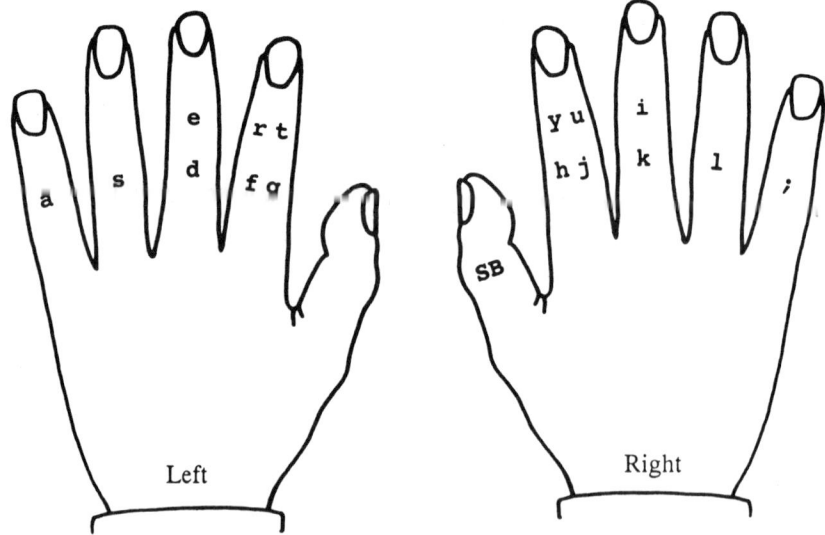

Set the margins at 12 and 72.

Practise these new letters using the fingers indicated. Say each letter to yourself as you strike the keyboard.

Type the following groups at least 5 times.

GROUP A

ed rf tg yh uj ik ed rf tg yh uj ik
ed rf tg yh uj ik ed rf tg yh uj ik

GROUP B

ed rft fgf ik ujy jhj ed rft fgf ik ujy jhj
de fg tf rf jh jy ju ik ed ik fr uj tf jy gf hj

GROUP C

edrf tfgf ikuj yjhj edrf tfgf ikuj yjhj
defg tfrf jhjy juik edik rfuj tfjt gfhj

GROUP D

ghdk eiru tyki dkei fjur fjg hyr
druj yghg jfru hkdi ertu ikd fed

Type each of the following sentences 3 times across the page, without looking at the keyboard. Remember to leave double line spacing (two carriage returns) after each group and to check your work carefully before attempting the next group. If you have more than 3 errors in a line, repeat it.

```
the red kite
the free gift
they tried it

their kite did fly
feed the deer
they freed her

they did judge her
there he hid
the grey teddy

they liked the fair
read the list
fill the flasks

he is a fidget
use the faster slide
fly daily; they said

the jute leaf;
read the list;
the tea is his
```

```
yesterday the girl had a salad
fudge has a great taste
faster; faster they yelled
get the details after

she ate the tasty fruit tart
high flyers get great deals
try the larger red jug; he said
he had asked his dad first
```

REMINDER

When inserting a fresh sheet of paper, make sure that the left edge is in line with the paper feed guide which should be set at 0. If the paper is not straight, use the paper release lever in order to correct it.

Always leave top and bottom margins of approximately 25 mm (7 lines).

Numbers **3, 4, 5, 6, 7, 8** can now be introduced. Note the fingering. Write them on your diagram.

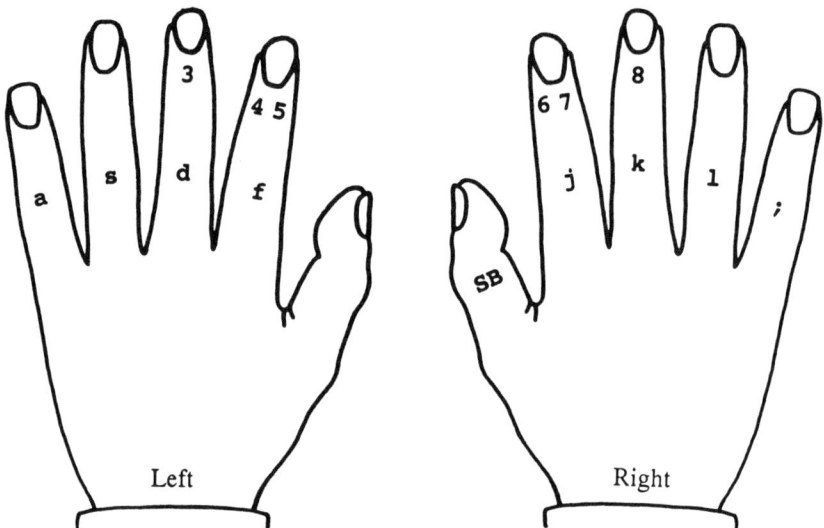

Type the following groups at least 5 times. (You may find that you have to glance at the keyboard when typing numbers.)

 Use margins of 12 and 72.

GROUP A

d3d 3d3 f4f 4f4 f5f 5f5
j6j 6j6 j7j 7j7 k8k 8k8

GROUP B

d3k8 d3k8 f4j7 f4j7 f5j6 f5j6

Type these sentences in the same format as before, remembering to check your work carefully. This is known as 'proof reading'.

```
6 fitted the seat
7 dusted the ledge
eat the 5 fresh fruits

5 hiked at the seaside
4 flutes; 3 guitars
6 lifted the huge fish
3 grey seals ate the fish

see 84 flags fly
the 67 kegs are full
the lad has 3 sisters
5 skaters skated here

they liked the 3 red dresses
58 reels are left; she said
65 is the age he retires
the guard had 75 keys

the lad juggled 8 eggs; he let 3 fall
the gales raged at the seaside
it is just like her said the girl sadly
the giraffe ate grass; the geese ate seeds
```

UNIT 3   New keys: v b   n m

Overview

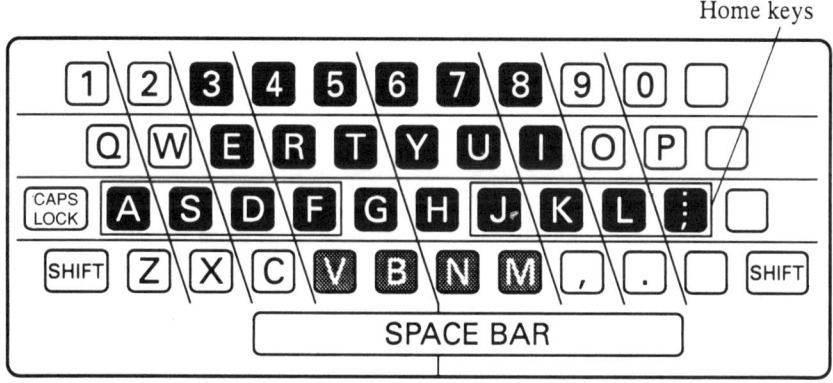

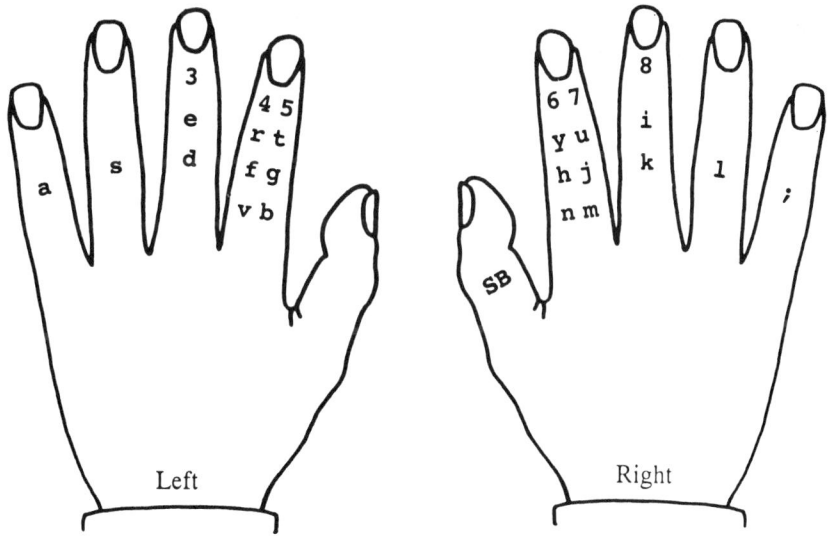

Left   Right

UNIT 3　New keys:　v b　n m

Add these to the diagram.

 Set your **margins** so that the left-hand margin is at 12 and the right-hand margin is at 72, giving a typing line of 60 spaces.

Home keys

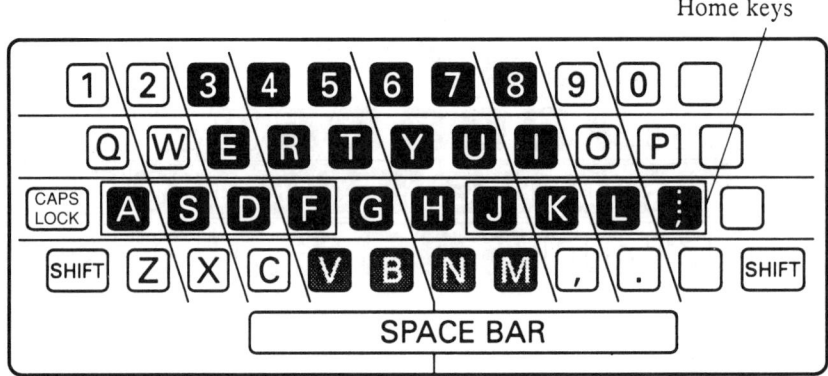

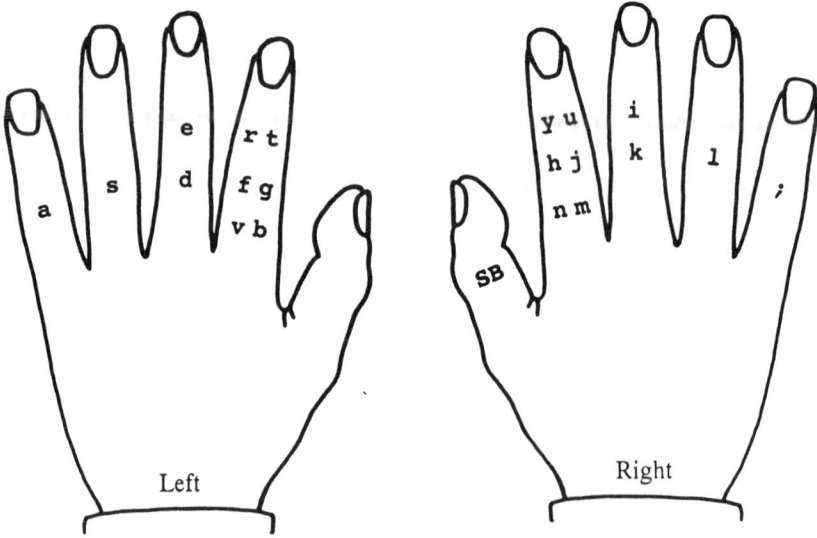

Left　　　　　　　　　　　Right

Practise these new letters, saying them to yourself as you strike the key. **Do not** look at your fingers, but refer to the diagram if necessary.

Type the following groups at least 5 times.

GROUP A

```
ed rfv tgb yhn ujm ik ed rfv tgb yhn ujm ik
ed rfv tgb yhn ujm ik ed rfv tgb yhn ujm ik
```

GROUP B

```
frfv frfb frfv frfb frfv frfb
jujm jujn jujm jujn jujm jujn
```

GROUP C

```
fvfg vgfb fgbg jmjh mhjn jhnh
fvjm fbjn fvfb jmjn gvgb jnjm
```

 Approximately 6/7 spaces before the right-hand margin setting, a bell will ring to indicate that you are near the end of the typing line.

Type these sentences 3 times across the page, checking your work carefully.

the merry men
hurry my friend
the bright blue jug

have a drink mate
these are big eggs
buy sugar and buns

see the brave girl
several sing hymns here
the train arrived late

the master taught them maths
find seven healthy animals
get high marks in the test

seventy fine trees in the valley
verify this statement sent by airmail
my trusted valet is retiring this year

the 7 drummers beat the rhythm steadily
the 3 small kittens tangled the string
they liked the 5 varieties they had at breakfast

the theatre had 8 seats available that night
at bedtime she liked a large milky drink in a mug
the silversmith made 6 beautiful silver rings
the valuable blue enamel jug fell 4 feet and smashed

REMINDER: Proof read your work and retype any sentence which contains more than 3 errors.

UNIT 4   New keys: c   ,
Overview

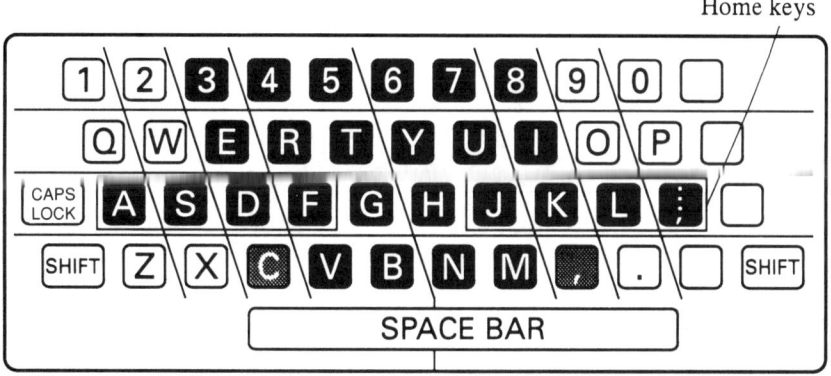

Home keys

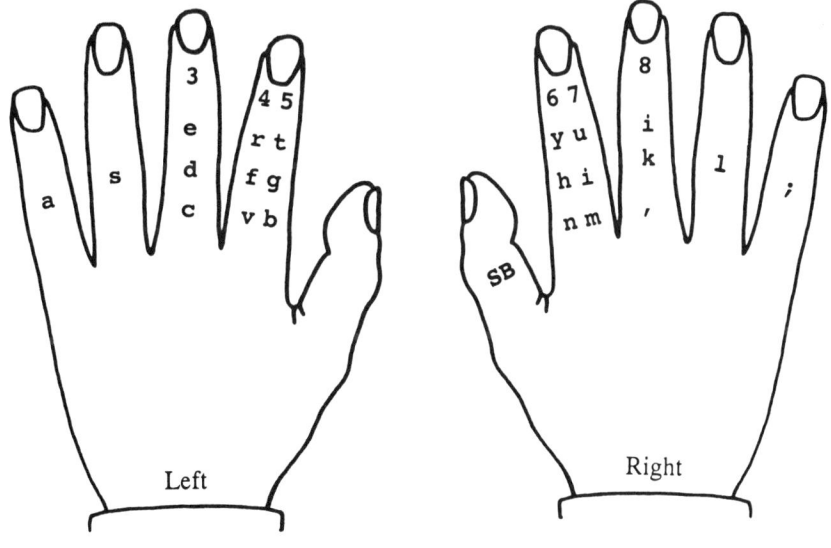

Left   Right

UNIT 4   New keys: c   ,

Add these to the diagram.

Before continuing, spend about 5 minutes practising the letters and numbers learnt in the previous Units.

Home keys

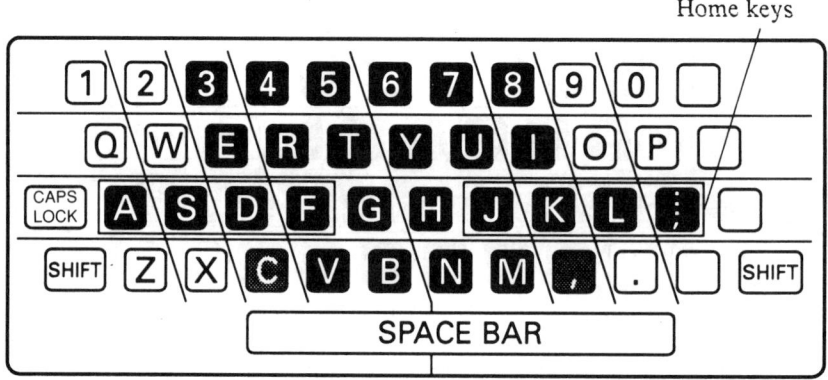

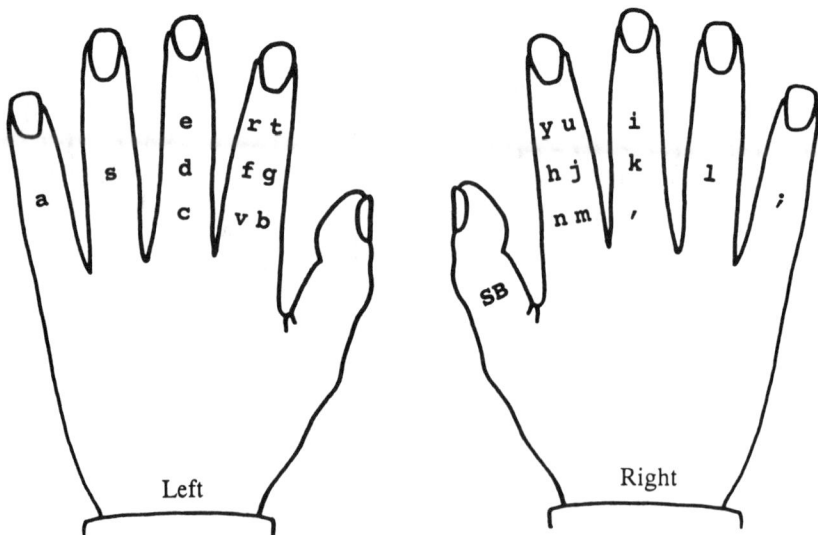

Left

Right

 Set the margins at 12 and 72, giving a typing line of 60 spaces.

NOTE

ALWAYS LEAVE ONE SPACE AFTER A COMMA.

Practise these new letters, typing each group 5 times.

GROUP A

```
edc rfv tgb yhn ujm ik, edc rfv tgb yhn ujm ik,
edc rfv tgb yhn ujm ik, edc rfv tgb yhn ujm ik,
```

GROUP B

```
edc dced ik, ki, ced, ki, dk, eic, ci,
k, cd edc ik, edc ik, cde, ki
```

GROUP C

```
edik bck, ed,k deki edik bck ed,k deki
eidk c,kd iekd ,cdk eidk c,kd iekd ,cdk
```

Type the following sentences, which incorporate all the keys learnt so far.
Type each sentence 3 times across the page.

 Set the margins at 18 and 78.

```
light the gas
guess the time
get the brave lad

he can fry the eggs
buy sugar, cakes and buns
birds fly and sing

the men ran in the rain
they take the night train
ten members in the band

find her, get them
several dreary days
find my red cardigan

they are mean and hungry
breakfast is very late;
he likes card games

clean the hall, then the table
he can dance, he can sing
lads and lasses danced all night

treat them nicely said her friend
sit in that mauve fireside chair
custard and cream cakes are fattening
the library shuts at lunch time every day
```

the hairdresser cut and styled my hair beautifully
buy beef and lamb at the butcher, as it is fresh daily
vegetarians eat beans, rice, cheese, eggs and nuts
her red geraniums are much better than last year

Are you confusing any letters? If so, repeat the relevant unit before continuing.

So far you have been typing in **single line spacing**.

 In order to type in **double line spacing**, look for the line spacer on your typewriter and move it to the number 2 setting.

 Alternatively, if you are using a wordprocessor, you will be able to format your document for double line spacing very easily. If in doubt, consult your manual.

7 just and true men debated the evidence in the case

8 lasses make fruit drinks during the break

3 and 7 are lucky ticket numbers in the raffle

be back by 6, the bus arrives 5 minutes later

4 very naughty lads grabbed the ladder and ran

there are 5 breakages because the vases crashed against the side

4 army generals led the brave men in the battle against the
enemy

treat them kindly, they had a bad time at the tennis match

may he have 74 nails, he can finish his difficult task then;

my friend had 8 creamy cakes, she gave me 3 and her sister 5

the 3 firemen held the ladder firmly and saved the tiny kitten

the audience in the theatre cheered the cast and the band

7 vegetables make a tasty salad dish in the summer time

the gardener dug a huge area, cut the grass and tidied the beds

3 mechanics mended my car, they sent me a huge bill yesterday

Check your work carefully, and repeat any sentences that contain more
than three errors.

UNIT 5   New keys: w x   o .   numbers: 2   9

Overview

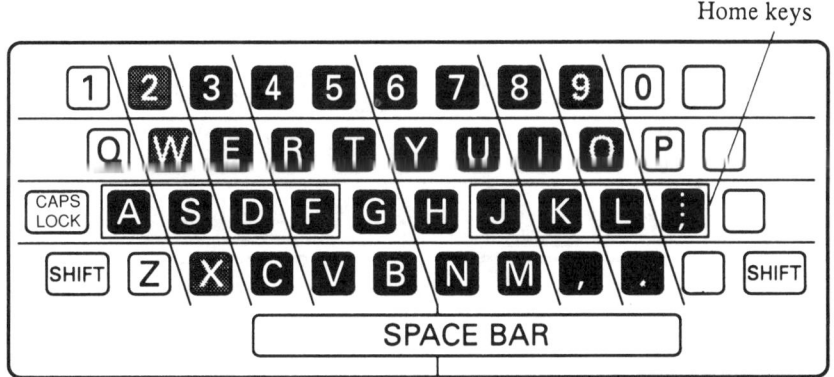

Home keys

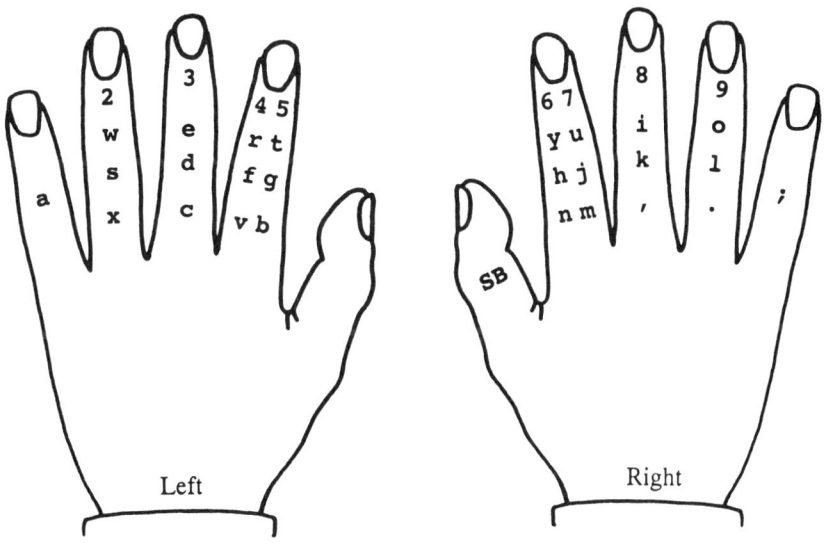

Left   Right

UNIT 5   New keys: w x   o .

Add these to the diagram.

Spend at least 5 minutes practising some of the sentences from the previous Units.

Home keys

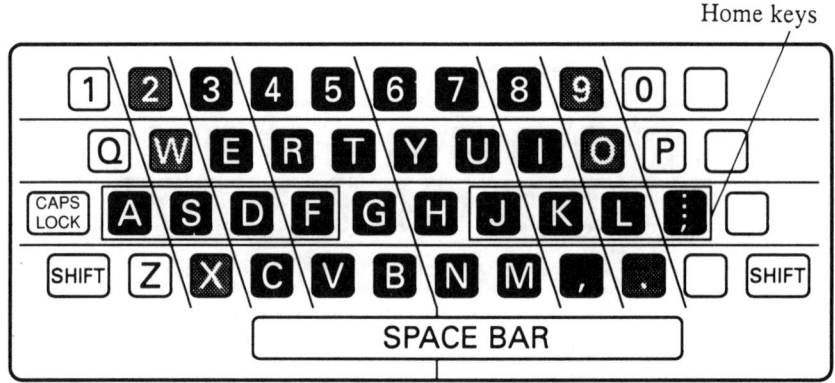

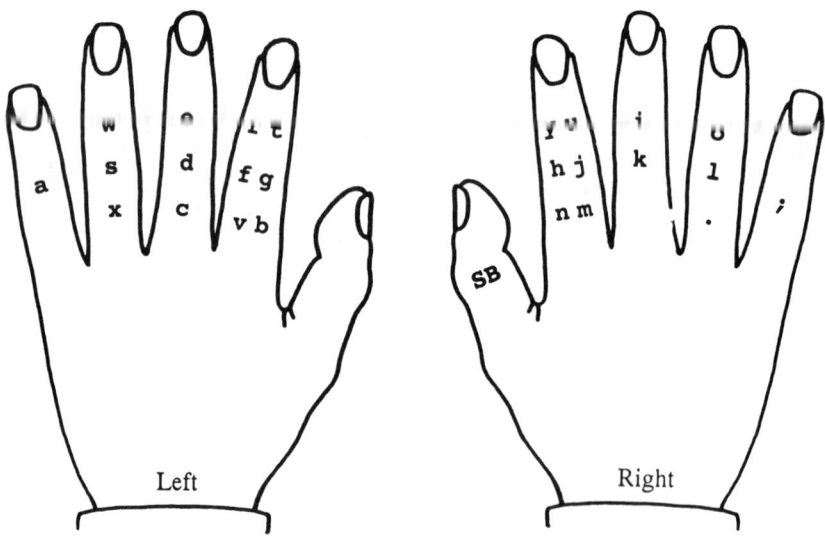

Left   Right

 Set your margins at 12 and 72 before starting to type.

NOTE

ALWAYS LEAVE TWO SPACES AFTER A FULL STOP.

Practise these new letters, typing each group 5 times.

GROUP A

wsx edc rfv tgb yhn ujm ik, ol. wsx edc rfv tgb yhn ujm ik, ol.
wsx edc rfv tgb yhn ujm ik, ol. wsx edc rfv tgb yhn ujm ik, ol.

GROUP B

xsw wsx xsw ol. lol. olo. xsw wsx xsw ol. lol. olo.
xsw wsx xsw ol. lol. olo. xsw wsx xsw ol. lol. olo.

GROUP C

swxlo. sox. xlw. wolx. swxlo. sox. xlw. wolx.
swxlo. sox. xlw. wolx. swxlo. sox. xlw. wolx.

Type the following sentences across the page. Each group should be typed three times accurately.

NOTE

REMEMBER THE CORRECT SPACING AFTER THE PUNCTU-ATION:

1 space after a comma or a semicolon.
2 spaces after a full stop.

 Set the margins at 18 and 82.

```
sixteen entered the race.
we sent them away.
milk is good for you.
```

```
clean the windows, they are dirty.
my car is yellow, your car is blue.
extra work is needed today.
```

```
your results are excellent.
just wait for the next bus.
tomorrow the sun will shine.
```

```
vitamins and minerals are good for you.
the bus was late, it had broken down.
when the clocks go back, winter is near.
```

in the summer we like to swim.
the bus was full this morning and so was the train.
strawberries, bananas and oranges are all sweet fruits.

the teacher marked the books, then wrote on the board.
their house was for sale; they bought a new bungalow.
the girl bought a balloon, but it blew away in the strong wind.

the swimmers won the race and were given a loud cheer.
their car broke down and had to be towed to the nearest garage.
are you checking your work before moving on to the next unit.

it is necessary to learn the keyboard thoroughly to ensure
accuracy.

most men retire at the age of sixty five, women usually retire
at sixty.

the children were allowed to watch the television, then they
did their homework.

nowadays dentists advise everyone to use fluoride, in one form
or another, and not to eat too many sweets.

Numbers **2** and **9** can now be introduced. Note the fingering and add them to the diagram.

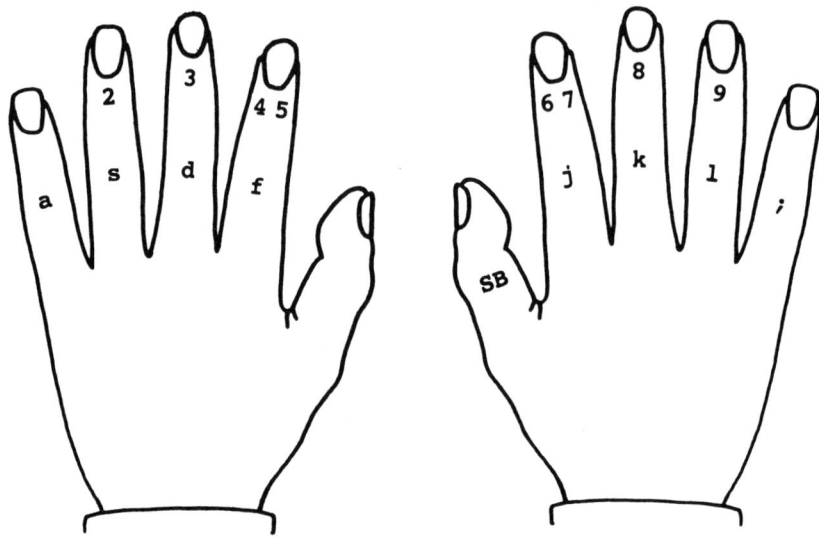

Type the following groups 5 times.

 Use margins of 18 and 82.

GROUP A

2wsx 9ol. 2wsx 9ol. 2wsx 9ol.
29xs 92lo 29xs 92lo s9l xo2 9s.

GROUP B

sx2s lo9. sx2s lo9. sx2s lo9.
sx2s lo9. sx2s lo9. sx2s lo9.

Now type the following groups of sentences three times across the page.

the girl ate 2 biscuits.
my house number is 82.
8 lasses make drinks.

the bus number is 29.
the hotel had 259 rooms.
the baker baked 99 small cakes.

the 6 chefs bake a 29th birthday cake.
the 4 girls danced in the ballet.
three times fifteen makes forty five.

24 hours in a day, 7 days in a week.
the 4 ducklings swam after their mother.
the monarch reigned for 9 years, then died.

Check your work carefully. Retype any sentences which contain errors.

UNIT 6 New keys: q z   p   numbers: 1   0

Overview

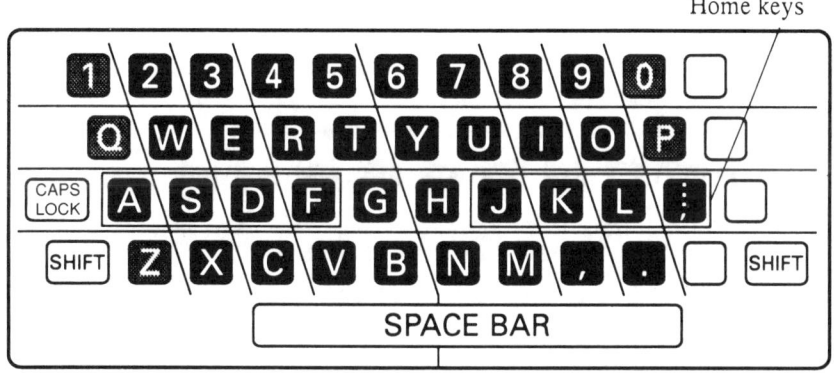

Home keys

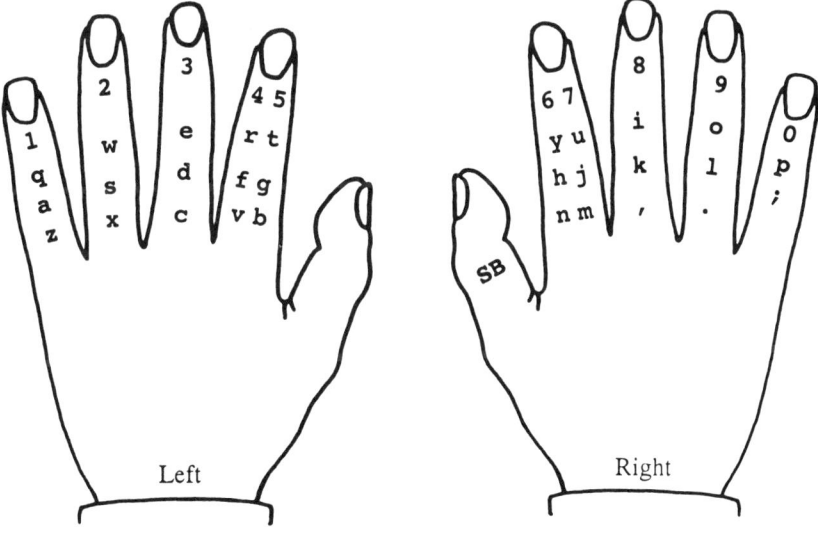

Left   Right

UNIT 6   New keys: q z   p

Add these final keys to the diagram.

Spend at least 5 minutes practising some sentences from the previous Units.

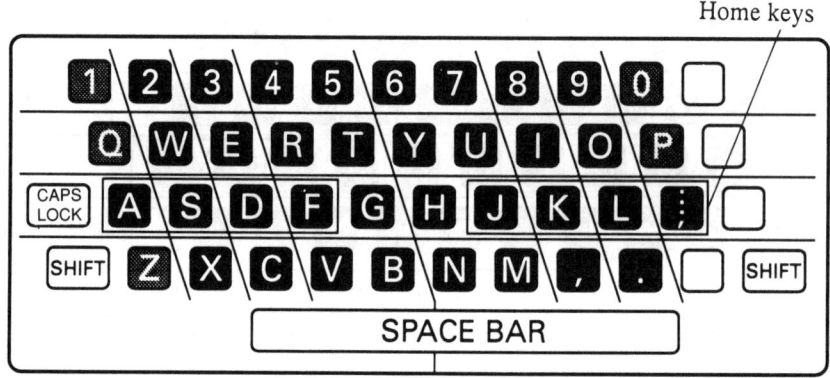

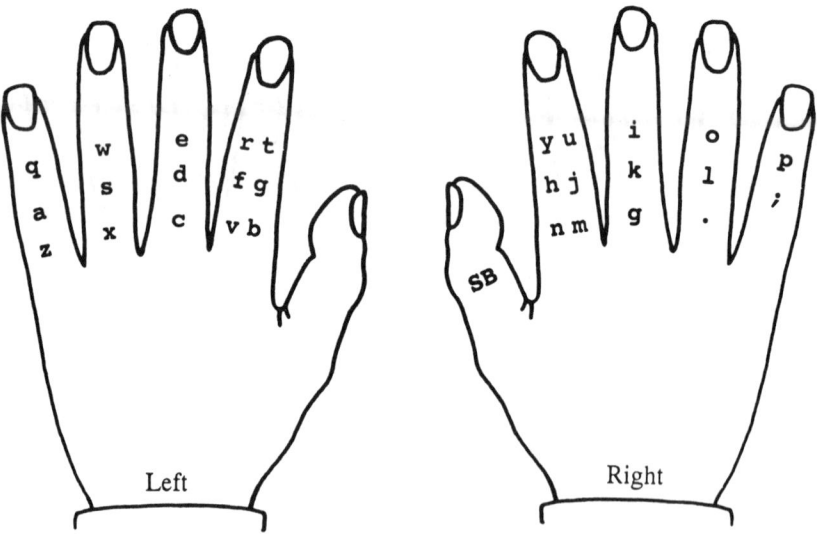

 Set your margins at 12 and 78 before starting to type.

Practise these letters, typing each group 5 times.

<u>GROUP A</u>

qaz wsx edc rfv tgb yhn ujm ik, ol. p;
qaz wsx edc rfv tgb yhn ujm ik, ol, p;

<u>GROUP B</u>

aqaz zaqa qza zqa p; ;p p; ;p p;
aqaz zaqa qza zqa p; ;p p; ;p p;

<u>GROUP C</u>

zqa p; aza p; apq; zpa pa; zqp aqpz;
zqa p; aza p; apq; zpa pa; zqp aqpz;

Set the margins at 20 and 80.

Type the following sentences accurately, three times each. Do not look at the keyboard; use the diagram for reference if necessary.

Proof read each group before going on to the next.

```
quick or you will be late.
quizzes are fun;
lazy souls lose out.

most children like the zoo.
we visited the castle.
the questionnaire was confusing.


the dancer hurt her foot.
play something on your saxophone.
equality does not always happen.


astronauts fly round the world quickly.
the rain went pitter patter on the window ledge.
the orchestra played some unusual music last week.


the teacher questioned the children about their projects.
the postman delivered the letters and parcels to the office.
the ozone layer is breaking down due to the greenhouse effect.
```

the newspaper quoted the exact speech made by the politician.
the lazy workman spent too long at his tea break.
the amateur dramatic society put on a very successful play.

small, local shops are having to close owing to the increase
in hypermarkets.

planning your summer holiday during the long, cold winter
nights can be fun.

the dressmaker made the young girl an exquisite ball gown to
wear to an important function.

board games used to be popular with children, but now computer
games have taken over.

the percussion section of the school orchestra were so
enthusiastic, the string section could not be heard.

the tramp pulled up his collar against the cold wind as he
trudged through the snowy streets of the city.

Numbers **1** and **0** can now be introduced. Note the fingering and add them to the diagram.

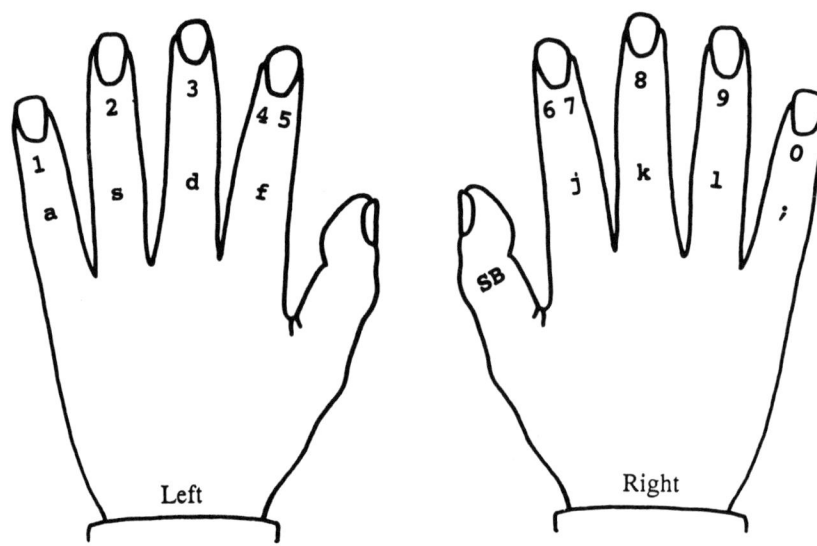

Left

Right

Type the following groups 5 times.

 Use margins of 18 and 82.

GROUP A

aq 1 qa 0p; aq 1 qa 0p; aq 1 qa 0p;
apq 1 0pa; 10a; qpz 0 q0 1; z; 01a;

GROUP B

1qa 0p; zal ;0p 1qa 0p; zal ;0p
10a; z01p qp10 zp01 10a z01p qp10 zp01

Now type the following groups of sentences three times across the page.

10 plus 10 equals 20.
the village had 193 inhabitants.
the dairy farmer kept 60 cows.

24 items make 2 dozen, not 3.
the television programme started at 6 pm.
his cheque for 30 pounds bounced.

the boat held 150 people.
10 gangsters robbed the bank.
100 years is a century, 10 years is a decade.

there are 7 days in a week and 365 days in a year.
if you use the 24 hour clock, 5.30 pm is 17.30.
a trio consists of 3 people, but a quartet has 4 people.

in most offices you will have a coffee break at 11 am, and a tea
break at 3.30 pm.

the boat leaves the quayside at 10.30 am and is due at its
destination 8 hours later.

the students will sit their examination on the 7th of next
month, in room 302 which is situated on the 3rd floor.

NOTE

Revise and retype the relevant unit if you are confusing any of the letters.

THE SHIFT KEY

When you need to type a capital letter, you use the **shift keys**. These are located on either side of the keyboard.

To type a capital letter with your **right hand**, you hold the **shift key** down with the little finger of your **left hand**.

To type a capital letter with your **left hand**, you hold the **shift key** down with the little finger of your **right hand**.

To type several capital letters, press the **caps lock key** on the left-hand side. This will **lock** the carriage into the 'upper case' position so you can type everything in **capital letters**.

Release by depressing either of the shift keys.

To cancel this command press the caps lock key again.

Capital letters are known as 'upper case' letters. 'Lower case' letters are the ones you have been typing.

Try typing these sentences, using the shift key for the capital letters. Remember to leave **two** spaces after a full stop.

Mary telephoned Jane on Wednesday. They arranged to meet.

This morning Helen was late for work. The bus broke down.

Paris is the capital of France. The Eiffel Tower is there.

Olga wrote poems in her spare time. Some were published.

Mr Downs lives in Northampton. He has a son in London.

A whale is a mammal, not a fish. There are many varieties.

The clouds floated in the sky. It was a lovely day.

Everyone likes summer holidays. The Mediterranean
area is popular.

The tea is kept in the blue jar. I keep the coffee in a red one.

Janice wrote a letter on Monday the 5th. A reply came on
the 8th.

As they walked across the field, they saw a notice BEWARE
OF BULL.

The Police sign said SLOW DOWN, as there had been an accident.

ALPHABETICAL SENTENCES

These sentences can be used whenever extra practice is needed.

Group 1

Amazing Amy ate apples and artichokes.

Brenda brought bananas in Bath.

Charlie can catch the Colchester Coach.

David dug the ditch down deep.

Each Easter we eat Easter eggs.

Fry the fish on Friday.

Get Greg to get the garnet.

Hilary has had her hair cut.

Isabel ironed her Italian shirt.

Judith and Julie ate junket and jelly.

Katie kindly cooked the cakes.

Lovely Laura lost her locket.

Michael marched magnificently on Monday.

Nervous Norman nearly always has nightmares.

Operatic Olivia opened the orange envelope.

Perhaps parrots perch on porches.

Quentin had a question for the Queen.

Rich Rosemary ran in the ruin.

Six soldiers sat still on the seat.

The turnips and tomatoes tasted terrific.

Unusual Ursula untied the umbrella.

Victoria and Victor voted against violence.

Wendy waved when William went away.

X films exclaims Xavier.

Yellow yachts you yelled.

Zealously, Zara organized the ozone friendly group.

Group 2

Ask Adam around this afternoon.

Buy bigger bottles of bleach for a better bargain.

Carefully Claire crossed at the crossing.

Drive down this dark road during the daytime.

Eat plenty of vegetables and eggs for extra energy.

Fifty four freckled frogs flopped into the pond.

Gold wrapping makes gifts look great.

Hedgehogs happily hibernate until it is hot.

I was interested so listened intently to the interviewer.

Justine juggles while the judges judge her jolly performance.

Kathleen knitted and the kitten knotted her wool.

Lemon or lime is lovely in a long cool drink.

Mincemeat and mashed potatoes make a meal.

Noisy neighbours are a nuisance at night time.

Oranges and olives grow in groves.

Potato patterns can be printed on paper.

Quotations are frequently used in quizzes.

Rain ran down the road in rivulets until it reached the river.

Snowdrops, sunflowers and several other species all smell sweet.

Under an umbrella is undoubtedly the best place to be in the rain.

Vacations or any variation in the routine are very invigorating.

When winkling at Whitstable be sure to wear waterproof wellies.

Exercise can be exhausting but exhilarating when executed daily.

Yesterday in York I saw a yellow yarn I would dearly like to buy.

Zany Zoe zig zagged all the way to the zoo.

Group 3

Able Amy asked Adam for an apple.

Buzzing bluebottles are beastly.

Christmas crackers cause considerable commotion.

Daring Doris dived to the depths.

Elizabeth eats eggs for energy.

Frances flew to France on Friday.

Go for gold was a good slogan.

Harriet had her hair highlighted.

In Italy Isabelle insisted on icecream.

January is when Judith juggles in her jacket.

Katie and Kevin were flying a kite in the park.

Laura looked longingly at the luscious lemon lolly.

Mary hummed musical melodies in the morning.

Naughty Nigel ignored the note Nora sent.

Only Oliver owned an orange grove.

Perhaps Peter can persuade Paula to play properly.

Quentin queued, then quickly went quietly home.

Rolls Royces are regal cars Rosemary said rapidly.

Simon stole the silver spoons on Saturday.

Trick or treat is talked about on the thirtieth.

Ursula was usually untidy but full of fun.

Vera had a very varied vocabulary which she used vociferously.

Winter woollies will wash well in cool water.

Excited Xavier was extraordinarily anxious.

Yesterday Yolande yodelled in York.

Zara saw a lazy zebra in the zoo.

Chapter 2
Fundamental Keyboarding Skills

KEYBOARDING SYMBOLS AND THEIR FUNCTIONS

There are several keys on the keyboard which you will not yet have used.

On the top line above each of the numbers you will find different symbols. Keyboards vary slightly and you should become familiar with the one you are using. All these symbols are obtained by using the **shift key**.

The opening and closing **brackets**, also known as **parentheses**, are situated next to each other. Information contained within the brackets is typed as follows.

(This is a sample of work typed in brackets.) Note that there is **no** space between the opening bracket and the word that follows, neither is there a space between the last word and the closing bracket. You only leave a space immediately before the opening bracket and immediately after the closing bracket.

This rule also applies to the **quotation marks**. 'Remember this golden rule' said the teacher.

£ = pound sign, typed immediately before the figure: e.g. £323.75.

@ = as at. An abbreviation usually found on invoices:
e.g. 24 @ 6p each = 144p.

% = percentage sign. Typed immediately after the figure: e.g. 25%.

& = This is known as the ampersand, an abbreviation for 'and'.

* = asterisk. Used to mark an item, usually indicating that there is a note about it at the foot of the page.

? = question mark. This is typed immediately after the last word of a sentence and therefore two spaces must be left after it, as in the case of a full stop.

/ = slash or oblique. No spaces are left either side of this: e.g. he/she.

$+$
$-$
$\times$ Mathematical symbols found on **most** keyboards. Always leave
$\div$ one space before and after any of these symbols: e.g. $2 + 8 = 10$.
$=$

Type these short passages which provide practice in the keyboarding symbols.

 Use A4 paper and set your left-hand margin at 15 and your right-hand margin at 85.

EXERCISE 1

"Come here quickly" said the man, "Otherwise the boy might drown, I don't think he can swim very well." The woman grabbed the rope and threw it to the lad. "Thanks" he said, "I can only swim 5 metres."

EXERCISE 2

The invoice showed that two tins of paint @ £3.50 each cost £7.00, the paintbrushes were £4.75 and the wallpaper was £6.99 per roll. As Jim needed 8 rolls of paper he had to pay £55.92 for his paper. His total bill came to £67.67 including VAT.

EXERCISE 3

The children's maths problems were:

16 + 23 = 39
34 − 12 = 22
98 x 20 = 1960
65 − 5 = 60
25% of 100 = 25

As they were clever children, they all got them right.

EXERCISE 4

The asterisk (*) is always typed immediately after the item
in the text. However, when used in conjunction with a
footnote you must leave 1 space after typing the asterisk.

eg Dear Sir or Madam*

Can you indicate which is more suitable Tuesday/Wednesday*.

* delete as applicable

Use A4 paper for these exercises. Set your left-hand margin at 12 and your right-hand margin at 78.

EXERCISE 5

The ampersand symbol (&) should never be used in the
"body" of a letter, however, it can be used in an address.

eg
Braithwaite & Sons
P W Waxwood & Co Ltd
Mr & Mrs F Bretton

EXERCISE 6

Many television programmes are interesting and/or
informative. Some programmes are entertaining, whilst
others are of no interest whatsoever. Have you ever watched
something that you have been totally bored with, but not
bothered to switch off?

EXERCISE 7

Dalmations (known to many of us as spotty dogs) are the breed
used in the children's film "101 Dalmations". This
popular children's film is also enjoyed by many parents
who remember it from their childhood days.

EXERCISE 8

Many forms to be filled in now have the addition of Ms to them. For example, one may find a form with Mr/Mrs/Miss/Ms on it nowadays.

The following words often cause problems in English grammar:

its/it's
there/their/they're
to/too/two

Do you know when to use each one of the above?

When you need to **underline (underscore)** any piece of work, a heading for example, use the underline facility.

 There is no need to turn the carriage up, simply backspace to the correct position. Here are a few _____ . Note how they join together and how the underlining sits below the line of type.

Never underscore punctuation marks and do not go beyond the typed characters.

Type the following: ''Now I can underscore''.

Look for another line on your keyboard. This is the **dash/hyphen**. Type several --------. Note the difference. There are spaces between each one and it is in the middle of the line of type - no good for underscoring!

When using this key as a dash, always leave a space either side of the symbol: e.g. The question is - what can we do?

When using the key as a hyphen, there are no spaces: e.g. make-up, deep-clean, up-to-date.

 Practise these exercises. Use A4 paper and margins of 20 and 80.

EXERCISE 1

The title of the book by Charles Dickens is <u>David Copperfield</u>. It is considered a <u>classic</u> and widely read. Everyone seems to enjoy this book however old they are.

EXERCISE 2

"Dash" - said Derek "I can't hyphenate this word."
"Yes you can" said Kelly, "you put the hyphen between the two consonants."

EXERCISE 3

Jim played cricket on the green last Sunday. He scored 142 runs and everyone congratulated him. He hopes he will be picked to be captain, but he will not know until David has decided. The next fixture will be on Saturday 14th June <u>NOT</u> Sunday 15th June.

EXERCISE 4

We had a delicious picnic, and it did not rain. "What a
surprise," Mary said loudly! Elizabeth suggested we go
again next Bank Holiday - let's hope we get good weather again.

EXERCISE 5

A lot of people would like to work part-time. Unfortunately
there are few good jobs available where this is possible -
perhaps more companies will consider this in the future.
Job-sharing is becoming more fashionable.

PARAGRAPHS

There are three different types of paragraphs: **blocked, indented** and
hanging.

The most widely used are the **blocked** style paragraphs. This is because
they are quicker and easier to type and have a much neater all round
appearance.

To distinguish between the end of one paragraph and the beginning of
the next, press the return/enter key twice to leave **one** clear line space.

BLOCKED STYLE

When typing in this style, every line must start at the left-hand margin. As you work through the book, you will notice that the majority of exercises are set out in the blocked style.

INDENTED STYLE

When typing work in this style, the first line is **indented** half an inch in from the left-hand margin. The remaining lines begin back at the margin.

Remember that when typing indented paragraphs, the first line of each new paragraph must be indented, and there must be one clear line space between each paragraph.

HANGING STYLE

'**Hanging**' paragraphs are so called because the first line 'hangs' over all the other lines.

Specifications and legal documents are often typed in this style as it is very distinctive.

 Use A4 paper and set your margins at 20 and 80.

Type the following short paragraphs; be sure to leave the correct spacing each time.

BLOCKED PARAGRAPHS

```
The holiday brochures, travel guides, etc are out now. Will
you decide to go ski-ing in the winter or choose to relax in
the Mediterranean sun?
```

On Wednesday 20 children visited the zoo. They saw lions, tigers and elephants. When their trip finished, they caught the bus home.

In winter the roads get icy and often the trucks are out sprinkling salt on the roads. Usually they miss my road, so I tend to slip all over the place.

In summer it is important not to burn in the sun. Too many people do not use a suitable sun protector, they just lie in the sun burning and turning bright red.

The builder decided to knock down the wall and put up a fence. The house owner was extremely annoyed as he did not want a wooden fence there.

The new Garden Centre which opened last week has been very busy. It sells all the usual plants and shrubs but also has a vast selection of patio furniture and barbecue equipment. There is a supervised play area for children, which means you can browse at your leisure.

The young girl was late for work as her train had been delayed due to points failure. It was the third time this had happened in two weeks and she was very cross.

To be skilled in typewriting it is necessary to practise regularly. Repeating sentences can be tedious but it is essential in order to become a fast and accurate touch typist.

When you have learned to type you will have acquired a skill. This new skill will enable you to get a better job or go on to learn word processing. Some people find it easier to learn to type than do others, eg pianists.

Accuracy is the most vital factor in typing. Do not assume that a fast typist is a good typist. The good typist is the one who concentrates on being accurate and as a result steadily builds up a reasonable speed, becoming even faster as confidence grows.

INDENTED PARAGRAPHS

Set a tab.

Use the indent facility.

Everyone says smoking and drinking are not good for you, but eating too much can also do you harm. Regular exercise is often recommended but it should not be too strenuous if you have not exercised for many years.

Typewriters have advanced greatly. The old manuals have become collectors' items; electric machines are not often used either. Nowadays electronic typewriters have taken their place. They have numerous time-saving functions; self-correcting and automatic centring are two such facilities.

The attendance at evening classes has increased dramatically in recent years. The variety of subjects covered has also risen. It is now possible to learn anything from making silk flowers to speaking a foreign language, car maintenance to Cordon Bleu cookery.

HANGING PARAGRAPHS

Use margin release and backspace 2.

Use the indent facility.

We are in the process of seeking ways to improve the range of services we offer to the public. We aim to save you money and make transactions as simple and easy as possible. As solicitors we put our client's interests first and offer a skilled, professional service.
Please contact any number of our experienced staff at either our London or Liverpool office.

Estate agents often use the hanging style of paragraphs because they can then position a picture of the house they are selling in the space left. Obviously they leave more than 2 spaces before typing the details. If you choose to work in an estate agent's office they will tell you how they like their work set out.

DID YOUR PARAGRAPHS TURN OUT CORRECTLY? CHECK YOUR WORK AND RETYPE ANY THAT CONTAIN ERRORS.

COPY TYPING EXERCISES

Now that you have learnt the keyboard, you must practise accurate copy typing before continuing.

Once you have typed an exercise, proof read it and if you have more than 5 errors retype it. If you make the same error each time, turn to the page that introduced the letter and just type through the sentences again.

 Set your left-hand margin at 15 and your right-hand margin at 85. Type the following in double line spacing. Remember to turn up twice between each paragraph (this also applies when typing in double line spacing.)

EXERCISE 1

Nowadays electronic typewriters are equipped with a correcting tape enabling errors to be easily dealt with.

A correcting ribbon in your machine means that on top copies the correction is 'clean'. However, all carbon copies must be corrected neatly and cleanly also.

If you use white fluid to cover up your errors, ensure that the liquid has dried before retyping anything otherwise you will just have a blurred imprint. Using a pencil rubber is another way of correcting any errors. Care must be taken to ensure that the surface of the paper is not rubbed away and that holes do not appear on the page. It is a good idea to place a piece of paper behind the carbon paper so that your copy is not smudged.

Careful erasing of any type is something you must learn to do neatly.

EXERCISE 2

Set your margins at 35 mm each side. Type in double line spacing.

Valentine's Day is a time when everyone feels a little romantic. Even the hardest-hearted soul takes a second look at the post in the hope that there will be something there.

The exchanging of tokens on Valentine's Day goes back to the Middle Ages. By the end of the 18th century the tradition had become formalized into the sending of love letters and poetry. These letters were often hand-painted and invariably hand-made.

As the sending of Valentines became more popular, cards were manufactured in quantity. Manufacturers became competitive and cards became more lavish, using silk, lace, tinsel and feathers. Even the envelopes were decorated to match their contents.

Today, the cards we can buy are not quite as glamorous but the tradition of sending tokens of love carries on.

EXERCISE 3

Set your margins at 35 mm each side. Type in double line spacing.

INTERVIEWING TIPS

When you go for an interview it is important to arrive in good
time. Make allowances for delayed trains or buses or parking
spaces. Find out exactly where you need to go so that you don't
get lost and arrive in a panicky state.

Make a note of any questions you would like to ask, for example
working conditions, promotion prospects, holiday
entitlement and, of course, salary. It is a good idea to find
out a little about the company as this shows you are interested
in the firm that may be your next employer.

Have your CV (curriculum vitae) to hand and up-to-date,
together with any other documents you have been asked to bring
with you. Be suitably dressed, remember that a neat and tidy
appearance will say a lot about your general character. You
will also feel more confident knowing that you have taken
trouble to ensure that you are well groomed. You are bound
to be nervous, but try to be as natural and relaxed as you
possibly can.

If you take note of this advice, it will help you to secure
the job of your choice.

EXERCISE 4

Type the following passage in double line spacing. Margins to be set at 35 mm each side.

Thousands of animals suffer and die in research laboratories because they are used to test cosmetics and toiletries such as lipsticks, soaps and shampoos. Many of the products which we use or wear every day of our lives have been paid for by their suffering.

Many companies have rejected crude, cruel tests such as the dripping of substances into the unprotected eyes of rabbits, in favour of safe and sensible alternative methods. Trials are conducted on human volunteers and also by using cell culture techniques.

It was only due to a huge public outcry and a massive publicity campaign on the part of animal rights organisations that proposals to increase the number of animals used in tests were defeated.

It is hoped that in the very near future these cruel tests will be officially banned, thus saving thousands of helpless animals.

EXERCISE 5

Type this exercise in single line spacing. Use suitable margins.

If you live in the south-east of England, an interesting and enjoyable day out can be a visit to France. This is not as expensive as you may at first think as you can take advantage of the many special offers that are around during the off-peak time of the year.

Part of the excitement of the day is the actual journey across the Channel. You can choose either the ferry or the hovercraft. Whilst the hovercraft is slightly quicker, it is quite noisy and you are not able to stroll around. The ferry will allow you to wander around, relax on the deck (weather permitting) and even have a meal.

When you arrive in France you can walk around the town, taking notice of the different shops - the cake shops, or patisseries as they are called, have the most wonderful displays of mouth-watering cakes. Test your knowledge of French by ordering something to eat or drink in a restaurant. You may wish to explore some of the historical sights and buildings before you head for the ever popular hypermarkets.

Once you return home, you can relive your day out when you sample the delicious French bread, cheese and wine purchased.

EXERCISE 6

Type this exercise in single line spacing, use suitable margins. Refer to Chapter 4 (General Typing Information).

Use A5 landscape paper.

Peter and Kim had made arrangements to go to the theatre that evening. Unfortunately, a delay at the station - due to the cancellation of the 6 o'clock train - meant that they were going to be late for the show.

Kim was extremely upset as she had been looking forward to this night out for some time. The play was a murder plot and they knew they would not understand it fully if they missed the first part. They arrived at the theatre in a complete panic, only to discover a large notice saying, "OWING TO TRAIN CANCELLATION THE SHOW WILL START 30 MINUTES LATER!"

PRINTERS' CORRECTION SIGNS

Work is often presented in a rough form containing errors and alterations. Work that has been drafted by hand is known as 'manuscript'. As the typist, you will be expected to reproduce an accurate type-written copy of the work in the correct format.

The writer of the document will indicate the alterations using standard printers' correction signs. Refer to Chapter 4 (General Keyboarding Information), which contains a list of those most commonly used.

As a general rule, the alteration will be indicated in the margin alongside the line containing the word/s to be altered, which will also be marked. The information given in the margin indicates the type of correction/alteration to be made.

The following gives examples of some correction signs together with a corrected version.

trs. It is important that you learn to recognise the most
uc commonly used Printers' Correction Signs. it is often
difficult to type from hand written work, especially if
Lc the writing is messy and the Work is full of alterations.
NP [The Correction Signs simplify and condense instructions
from the writer.

It is important that you learn to recognise the most commonly used Printers' Correction Signs. It is often difficult to type from hand written work, especially if the writing is messy and the work is full of alterations.

The Correction Signs simplify and condense instructions from the writer.

EXERCISE 1

Use of Printers' Correction Signs.

Now that you have learnt the correcting signs, correct this   *trs*
exercise carefully. make sure that you do not miss anything   *uc*
and that you proof read your work afterwards. Sometimes work
may be given to you to type and later returned with correction
signs marked.

It would be quite annoying to find that you had forgotten some   *#*
of these, especially if you were working for someone high up
L   in the company. Notice that this item is typed in ~~double~~ single line   *# Ⓛ*
spacing throughout. This is so that the printer's ~~correction~~   *⊃ 7*
or manuscript corrections can be seen easily.

EXERCISE 2

Hotel work c/an be very exciting especially if you like   *7*
working with people. it can be tiring as you never know if you   *# uc*
will have to work late or not. Generally though life in hotels   *Lc*
is very rewarding. Perhaps you will have the opportunity to
travel abroad especially if you work for an International
company. [Some people can be very pleasant, but others are   *NP*
quite rude and short-tempered. You will have to be courteous
to every one if you decide to work in an hotel.   *⊃*

EXERCISE 3

Type a corrected version of the following.

In 1900 a woman's lot was not a happy one. Women did not have the vote, which meant they had no voice, no rights and no way

N.P of changing their lives. // Many literally worked for a pittance, in sweat factories, in kitchens, indeed, anywhere they could get

✓ employment. With no voice they were often at the whim of unscrupulous employers.

CAPS In 1918 this changed

NP After all the years of fighting and cajoling, Mrs Pankhurst and

uc the suffragettes won the day. Women were at long last given the vote.

EXERCISE 4

Type a corrected version of the following.

Part-time classes, whether day or evening, are most enjoyable.

You can meet new friends and learn new skills.

It must be remembered that you may well have to pay additional costs for your materials, such as
trs books/and paper. In most instances you will be told how much extra
✓ this will be ~~on~~ *during* your first lesson.

Some times students are interested
uc in Flexistudy. this system enables those students whose working hours do not fit in with College hours,
∩ to study as and when they can. They still have contact with their
NP tutors. // The majority of Colleges have access for special needs students and welcome them.

USE OF ABBREVIATIONS

Refer to the list of 'Commonly used abbreviations' in Chapter 4 (General Keyboarding Information) before typing the following exercises.

EXERCISE 5

With ref to the catalogues we have just recd, we wd like to advise you of the results. The adverts were very good and we can send the draft off to the printer immed.

Obviously we would like the copies returned promptly so that the temp secs can have the relevant work as soon as poss.

The a/cs ctte wl have to decide whether the project is within the business budget. We def want to dev the new idea & need to fix appts with those resp in order to give them all the necy info.

Let me know if you wl be able to attend the meeting next Thurs. If this is incon, telephone me by Tues.

EXERCISE 6

We ack rec of yr letter. The accom you require for your colleagues wl be available on Mon/Tues the 24/25 Feb.

As mentioned, it wl be necy to send a deposit so that we can gntee your booking wl be held. As requested, I enc a copy of next year's brochure tog w the price list which is effective from Jan 1st.

EXERCISE 7

The suppliers hv let us down w the del of bldg materials needed to complete the site on the New North Road. They say their mfrs are experiencing difficulty with obtaining clearance of the goods from Holland - they are held up in the Customs Dept at Dover.

However, there is suff work for approx 10 of the men at our housing estate project in Enfield. The rest of the work-force I am afraid will have to be laid off until further notice, they shd meanwhile submit last week's travel exps claim form.

PROOF READING

Proof reading means checking your work carefully for any errors. This should be done **before** removing the work from the machine as it can be difficult to line work up once it has been taken out of the typewriter. You should get into the habit of checking all your work very thoroughly, not only for typing errors but also for consistency in style.

The following 6 exercises each contain ten errors. Circle or underline them and then type a corrected version.

EXERCISE 1

A word proccessor is an automatic typewriter that can do a wide vareity of things.
Word processors consist of a keyboard - similer to a typewriter keyboard, a printer, a screen which is known as a VDU, a memory facility & a storage unit. the storage is usually on a disc

The benifits of a word processor are that they save time, especialy if there are errors to correct. If you were using a WP now and you made an error, you would not have to correct your top copy or retype it. You could just make the alteration on teh screen, and print out a correct version.

EXERCISE 2

When using the telefone you must always answer in a clear way.
You should give the number and not just say "hello". keep a
pencil and notpad buy the telephone so that you can take an
message or details of the caller.

Always be polite and helpfull. If you are the
receptoinist you are the first contact and the way you answere
is importent.

EXERCISE 3

Are you enjoying typing? Their is a lot to learn- as I expect
you have found out. Now that you have learnt the keyboard,
paragraping, printer's correctoin signs and How to proof
read, you are ready too progress to the different sections
where you will learn how to set out letters and memmos. You
will aslo learn how to display you work correctly.

EXERCISE 4

during the light summer evenings one does not need to use tthe
lights on a bicycle as cyclists can easily bee seen. However,
as the long winter nihgts approach it is essential to have
front and rear lampes. Too often cyclists Forget to check
the batteries and may, indeed, think the lamps are working
when in in fact, they are not. Thus puting themselves at great
risk

EXERCISE 5

At a Fitnesss Testing Centre you will be mesured in height and girth. You will be weighed and have your blood pressure taken- all by trained staff. Acording to the results you will be gived special diet sheets and excercises to help you acquire the desired level fo fitness.

You mus expect to put alot of effort, one way or another, in to to working towards you goal.

EXERCISE 6

London Transport will do anthing to make passenger's lives more cheerful, except cut fairs. Latest in along line of innovations are sixteen shop-linker busses which come into service next year.

In order to distinguish these buses from the normal service, they will be painted in red and yelow and there bus stops will have special red and yellow symbles.

These buses will travel ona circular route serving all the main shops in Regent Street, Oxford Street Knightsbridge and kensington.

Chapter 3
Document Presentation

This chapter is divided into the different typing topics necessary for you to become efficient in producing business documents.

Each topic is fully explained and backed up with an example. Several practical exercises are given within each section.

This chapter contains the following topics:

Letters
    A5/A4
    Circular
    Form

Envelopes

Centring/Display

Memoranda

Tabulation/Tables
    Basic
    Boxed (ruled)

Forms
    Preparation
    Completion

Business documents
    Curriculum vitae
    Itineraries
    Notice of meetings
    Agendas
    Minutes

LETTERS (INTRODUCTION)

All companies will expect their office staff to produce 'mailable' work; i.e. the work must be accurate, neat and clean as it is a representation of the company. There is a basic format which most companies use.

A **business letter** is made up of the following:

Reference	Used to trace and/or file correspondence. Usually consisting of initials of person sending letter and person typing letter.
Date	All letters must be dated. It is usual to type DAY MONTH YEAR in that order.
Addressee	The name and address of the person/company the letter is being sent to.
Salutation	The words 'Dear Sir', 'Dear Madam', 'Dear Mr', 'Dear Mrs', 'Dear Miss', at the start of the letter.
Body of letter	This is the actual letter. Generally typed in single line spacing with double line spacing between the paragraphs. This part of the letter is **always** punctuated.
Complimentary close	The 'ending' of the letter. 'Yours faithfully', for letters starting with 'Dear Sir/Madam'. 'Yours sincerely', for letters starting with 'Dear Mr/Mrs/Miss'.
Name of firm	When shown, typed directly under the complimentary close in capital letters.

Name of person signing letter	The name of this person is typed 6 lines below the 'complimentary close' - or name of firm if this is shown. 6 lines are left so that the person has plenty of room to sign the letter.
Designation	The position of the person signing the letter. Sometimes this is not required.
Enclosure/Attached	If anything is to be enclosed with the letter, this is indicated by typing 'enc' 3 lines below the last item typed. 'Attached' is indicated by typing 'att'.

Prepare this **sample letter**.

Before typing the word 'Reference', turn up 10 lines to represent the letter heading, or 2 lines below the heading if you are using headed paper.

This example indicates the correct spacing when typing a letter:

Use A5 portrait style paper. See Chapter 4 (General Keyboarding Information) for paper sizes. Use margins of 16 and 56.

Reference *-enter/return twice*

Today's date *-enter/return twice*

Name
and address
of person letter
is being sent to *-enter/return twice*

Dear Sir/Madam

You should use block paragraphs in the fully-blocked letter. Remember to turn up two lines between paragraphs.

As every line starts at the left-hand margin, this type of letter is quicker and easier to type.

Whether your letter is typed on A4 or A5 paper, the spacing will remain the same. *-enter/return twice*

Yours faithfully
NAME OF FIRM SENDING LETTER *-enter/return 6 times*

Name of person signing letter
Job of person signing letter

Prepare the following **letter** which uses **open** punctuation. Remember to use the correct spacing as shown in the previous example.

 Use A5 portrait style paper and margins of 16 and 56.

Ref RW/1

(Date)

Mrs M Smith
24 The Avenue
New Town
NT1 2XY

Dear Mrs Smith

This is an example of a letter in the open punctuation style. You will notice that there is no punctuation in the reference, date or name and address, neither is there a comma after "Dear Mrs Smith", or "Yours sincerely".

However, it is most important that you remember to punctuate the actual information contained in the letter. This is because the sense of the letter must not be altered.

Open punctuation is more widely used nowadays as it gives a clearer and sharper appearance. Compare it with the example on the following page, which uses standard punctuation.

Yours sincerely

Roger Winter
Business Studies Department

Prepare this **letter**, which uses **standard** punctuation. Remember to use the correct spacing as shown on the previous letters.

 Use A5 portrait paper and margins of 16 and 56.

Ref: LW/2

(Date)

Mrs. M. Smith,
24, The Avenue,
New Town,
NT1 2XY.

Dear Mrs. Smith,

Here is a letter typed in the fully-blocked style, using standard punctuation.

It is important to remember that if you begin your letter in this style you cannot switch to open punctuation half way through and vice versa.

Standard punctuation is very rarely used nowadays when typing business letters.

Your sincerely,

L.W. Winter,
Administration Officer.

ENVELOPES

When preparing envelopes, the name and address **must** be typed in exactly the same way as they appear on the letter, i.e. open/standard punctuation.

To position the name and address it is easiest to remember to come in one-third of the length of the envelope, and come down two thirds from the top edge (usually about 13 lines).

The words 'Confidential', 'Private', 'For the attention of', 'By hand', are typed two lines above the name and address.

CONFIDENTIAL

The Managing Director
Waxwood & Co Ltd
St Georges Mansion
726 Conway Avenue
London
W14 7AB

If you do not have an envelope to hand, you can fold a piece of A4 paper in half, and then in half again to make A6 size, or fold your A4 paper into 3 keeping the wider edge at the top.

Try typing your own name and address as though you were addressing an envelope yourself. When you have successfully typed your envelope, try these addresses:

1 Mrs M King 24 Hillcrest Northampton NT5 6PJ

2 Worth and Sons Ltd. St. Gerards House, 267 Great Street, Manchester, M67 8RE.

3   Confidential Miss S Grasse 5 Farbank Drive Glasgow G46 7SC

4   **For the attention of Mr G Kempton Quickfast Printing plc 38 Havelock Road Luton LU7 4TN**

5   Private Mr L Corbett Managing Director Exotic Foods plc Kingston House Southend Road SE67 1MC

6   BY HAND. Mrs. J. Dodman, Headmistress, Hamford School, Hamford, Essex. ES2 6BJ.

LETTERS (PRACTICE)

EXERCISE 1

Prepare the following letter using **open punctuation**. Use today's date.

 Use A5 portrait style paper.

Ms F Clarke
Building Dept
28 Sandhurst Avenue
Norwich
NR5 2PT

Dear Ms Clarke

Thank you for your recent letter.

I can now confirm that we shall not continue with the leasing
of the warehouse facilities due to the increase in rent.

In view of this our Warehouse Manager will be contacting you
to arrange for the transfer of any outstanding stock.

Yours sincerely

P Goodsen
DIRECTOR

EXERCISE 2

Prepare the following letter, remembering to use the correct layout and the current date.

 Set margins at 12 and 58. Use A5 portrait style paper.

```
Mrs D Avis 49 Crane Grove London N8 7LB

Dear Mrs Avis

Further to your telephone enquiry, I am pleased to advise you
that the dress you require is now in stock.

On receipt of your cheque for £47.70 (this includes postage
and packing), we will immediately despatch your dress to you.

Yours sincerely
LINDSEY FASHIONS PLC
```

EXERCISE 3

Key in this letter using suitable margins and today's date. Prepare an envelope to accompany the letter.

Miss M Booth National Stores plc High Holborn London WC1 1CW

Ref WP/your initials

Dear Miss Booth

We very much enjoyed your careers talk on the role of the Personnel Officer.

The girls appreciated the time and trouble you took to answer all their numerous questions and for all the advice you gave them.

The booklet entitled "The Personnel Officer Today" has proved to be very useful in our follow-up discussions in the careers lesson.

Yours sincerely

Wendy Payne
Careers Officer

EXERCISE 4

 Prepare this letter together with an envelope.

Mr P Briggs 25 Westward Close Wiltshire 3NB 4SG

Ref L1/5672/ your initials

Dear Mr Briggs

You may be aware that our new "Wheelybin" dustbins are being introduced to your street next month.

We have found that once householders become used to these new bins they much prefer them to the old system . We would ask you to continue to place your refuse in a bag before putting it in the Wheelybin for hygienic reasons.

Thank you for your co-operation.

Yours sincerely
TOWN CLERK

EXERCISE 5

Prepare this letter with today's date.

 Use A4 paper. Set margins of 35 mm. Follow the line spacing given for A5 letters.

Mr M McGregor
J & P Printers Ltd
Northside House
887 Patchett Road
Surrey SY5 3OP

Dear Sir

I am writing with regard to your advertisement for P.A to your Sales Director.

At present I am employed by a large organisation as secretary to the Senior Partner. I have been with this company for the past 3 years, starting as a junior.

I enclose a copy of my C.V. together with photocopies of my certificates.

I look forward to hearing from you.

Yours faithfully

Carol Ferris

Encs

EXERCISE 6

Key in this A4 letter. Use suitable margins, today's date and type an envelope.

Ref MA / your initials

Miss Young
25 Albany Grove
Hatch End
HA2 8PL

Dear Miss Young

Following your interview with Mr McDonald last week, we have pleasure in offering you the post of Junior Secretary.

Your hours of work and salary are as discussed with Mr McDonald. Would you arrive at reception at 10.00 am on Monday 29 January where Miss Thompson will meet you and take you to your department.

We hope you enjoy working in our company with us.

Yours sincerely

Mary Armstrong
Personnel Officer

EXERCISE 7

Key in this A4 letter which contains some correction signs. Use suitable margins, today's date and type an envelope.

Ref MJ/your initials

Mr F Hill
89 Chester Court
Liverpool
LP8 5TR

Dear Mr Hill

Thank you for yr letter enquiring about our latest range of electrical lawn mowers.

run on We are introducing a completely new model which features a safety cut out uc device. this mower will be available at most garden stores in approx 6 weeks time, at a very competitive price. It is included in our cat which we are enclosing with this letter.

If you have any difficulty in obtaining any of these products, please contact me again.

Yrs scly

M Jones

Sales Promotion Adviser
LAWN MOWERS LTD
Enc

EXERCISE 8

Key in the following letter, together with an envelope.

 Use appropriate-sized paper and suitable margins.

Sunshine Holidays plc
Quayside House
Brighton Road
BN5 1JG

Dear Sir

uc   With ref to my holiday booking no 462 to Spain in August, I enclose my cheque

NP   for the deposit and holiday insurance. // I look forward to receiving the confirmation of my holiday, together with the insurance policy described in your brochure.

yrs ffly

Kathleen Jay

EXERCISE 9

This letter is to Mr R Green of 67 Allandale Road Little Plumpton
Oxford OX1 23J. Date for today and prepare an envelope.

Dear Mr Green

I note from your card in the newsagents in the High Street
that you are available for light gardening work.

I require someone on a twice weekly basis to maintain my front
and back gardens. If you are interested, please ring me on
Oxford 8492 after 5.00 any evening.

Yours sincerely

Angela Smedley

EXERCISE 10

Key in the following letter, together with an envelope.

Ms D Barrett 76 Marlborough Drive Glasgow GS4 8SC

Dear Madam

Thank you for returning the ~~sweater~~ jumper which you purchased recently. // We have noted your complaint which we feel is justified and are enclosing a refund for the amount paid, plus postage.

We hope that you find future purchases totally satisfactory.

Yours ffly

Customer Services Dept

Enc

EXERCISE 11

Use suitable margins, today's date, and type an envelope.

Mrs P Bond 35 Chancery Drive
Basingstoke BA4 07T

Dear Mrs Bond

Our records show that your contract for
the servicing of your washing machine
NP expires next month. // If you would
like to renew the existing contract,
please send us your cheque for £35
before the 30th of next month and
complete the enclosed renewal form.

Yrs sly

Westside Electrics Ltd

Enc

EXERCISE 12

Prepare this A4 letter, making the necessary corrections.

Mr M Stapleton
The Ride
Taunton
Devon DN7 3AD

Dear Sir

Congratulations – You have won 1st Prize trs of in the raffle recently held in at the uc Star hotel in Brighton.

⊘ Your lucky number was selected picked out by our computer's random number selection scheme at the hotel last week.

You may remember that the 1st Prize consisted of a free weekend in Paris for 2 people during April or May, either this year or next year, as well NP as £100 spending money. // Perhaps you would contact us and let us know when you would like to claim your prize.

Yours ffly

HOLIDAY PROMOTIONS

EXERCISE 13

Prepare this letter together with an envelope.

Mrs T Sinclair 10 Red Street Dover Kent

Dear Madam

We are pleased to inform you that the curtains you ordered from our soft furnishings department now await your collection.

We would be happy to deliver these goods if you so desire.

Yours faithfully

EXERCISE 14

Using suitable paper and margins, type the following letter. Use the current year for the date.

2 February . . . .

Elite Business College
22 Swansea Road
Preston PR1 2HS

Dear Sirs

I am writing to enquire if you have any vacancies on your Word Processor Course which is due to start in September.

I will be leaving school this summer and hope to eventually find employment as a secretary. I have already passed the elementary and intermediate typing exams and can take down shorthand at 70 wpm.

I look forward to hearing from you.

Yours faithfully

EXERCISE 15

Prepare this letter. Date for despatch tomorrow and prepare an envelope.

Ms F Clarke Building Dept 28 Sandhurst Ave Norwich NR5 2PT

Dear Ms Clarke

NP Thank you for yr recent letter. [I can now confirm that we shall not continue with the leasing of the warehouse facilities due to the increase in rent.

In view of this, our Warehouse Manager will be contacting you to arrange for the transfer of any outstanding stock.

yrs scly

P Goodsen

DIRECTOR

EXERCISE 16

Prepare this letter.

The Personnel Officer Wilson Brothers Unit 12 County Trading
Estate Field End Lane Milton Keynes MK3 2DN

Dear Sir/Madam

We are writing to you with regard to Mr Edward Mason who we
understand was employed by you for a number of years.

We would be grateful if you would give us a character reference
and also comment of his suitability to be employed as a quality
control manager in our factory.

Enclosed is an SAE for your reply.

Yours faithfully
STUDDALL PLASTICS PLC

EXERCISE 17

Prepare this letter.

Ref GW/own initials
(date)

Mrs M Shah 3 Beech Avenue Harrow HA1 2UW

Dear Madam

Thank you for yr letter which we received yesterday.

The catalogue you requested will not be in stock until the beg of next month. As soon as we receive our new stocks, we will send you a copy.

We are sure you will find many up to date styles in our cat at competitive prices, and look forward to receiving your order.

Yours ffly
Fashions plc

G Woodley
Customer Services

EXERCISE 18

Prepare this letter.

Ref MG/own initials
(date)

Mr Baxter 197 Green Street Norwich NR2 3LR

Dr Mr Baxter

ACCOUNT NO - DB/489/X

May we remind you that you have not yet settled your a/c for last month.

We are sure this is due to an oversight and we look forward to receiving your cheque by return.

If you have paid this bill within the last seven days, please disregard this letter.

Yours scly
Furnishing Co Ltd

M Gomez
Accounts Manager

EXERCISE 19

Prepare this A4 letter, making the necessary corrections. Type an envelope.

Ref 10/4/18947
Mrs J Patel 24 Portland Street
Manchester M1 3HU

Dear Mrs Patel

Claim No 18947/3

Further to our telephone conversation of 27th April, we have pleasure in enclosing a cheque in full settlement of your recent claim in respect of the
NP damage to your car. [We also confirm
uc that this will not affect your no claims
uc bonus.

yours sincerely

Anna Fitzgerald
Claims Dept

EXERCISE 20

Prepare this letter and type an envelope.

Mr T Hilton Universal House 6 Regency Gardens London 1A 9EJ

Dear Mr H

Thank you for yr letter wh I recd last week. I apologise for
the delay in answering, but I have just returned from my
holiday.

I wd like to confirm that we can meet your requirements by the
date agreed & I do not foresee any problems with future
delivery dates.

Yrs scly

Janet Montague

EXERCISE 21

Prepare this A4 letter with today's date. Make all the necessary corrections.

Miss C Dodman
1 Cherry Tree Lane
Coventry
CV4 2TL

Dear Miss D

trs   We were sorry to recieve your

(✓)   letter in which you ~~complain~~ state that you & your friend were unhappy with the accommodation offered to you on your recent holiday in

uc   marbella.

We have looked into all the points you raised and hope to rectify a lot of the problems in the near

cr   future. We have also ~~decided~~ contacted the hotel manager and

have↳ our representative & ↳ passed on your comments, to them. Meanwhile we hope you will accept the enclosed cheques for

stet   £100 each ~~by way of~~ in compensation and hope you will continue to use our company for your future holidays.

Yours sincerely
Keith Johnson
Customer Service Manager
Enc

EXERCISE 22

Prepare this A4 letter with an envelope. Make all the necessary corrections.

Ref LG/your initials

Ms Thelma Jacobs
The City College
Exeter EX2 1PT

Dr Ms Jacobs

WORK EXPERIENCE REPORT   u/score

Our company has not had secretarial students on work exp before & we were therefore unsure of what to expect.

Ann settled in very well, although at the beginning we felt that she was rather shy & lacked confidence. However, by the end of the fortnight with us she was

NP   much more self-assured. [We found Ann to be pleasant & helpful & we were pleased with her work especially her knowledge of the computer.

punctual

⊘   She was always on time & on two occasions offered to stay late to help

NP   out with urgent work. [We would be more than pleased to take another student next year.

Yrs scly

Lucie Gardiner

EXERCISE 23

Prepare this letter on suitable-sized paper, together with an envelope.

a/ For the attention of the Cookery Department
Modern Women Magazine
High Holborn
London
WC2 IEJ

Dear Sirs

stet As an avid reader of your most ~~enjoyable~~ excellent
magazine I was delighted to see, in a recent
edition, a recipe for a chocolate mousse
NP which contained a cream substitute. [I am
on a special dairy-free diet so I straight
away tried it out & found it was a huge
success. Unfortunately I seem to have mislaid
the magazine and cannot get hold of
NP another one in my local area. [Could you
please let me have a copy of the recipe
and I enclose a stamped addressed
envelope in anticipation

Yours ffly

Harriet Chalmers

Enc

EXERCISE 24

Prepare this letter with an envelope.

The Manager Everglades Hotel
Taunton Devon

Dr Sir

Your hotel has been recom to me by a friend who recently enjoyed a relaxing week with you.

I understand that at certain times of the year you offer special deals for families.

NP Would you please send me details of these offers. [Do you have any offers
UC for this coming easter break?

I look forward to hearing from you.

yrs ffly

Peter Watson

EXERCISE 25

Prepare this letter with an envelope.

Mrs M Lander
28 Westgate Square
Cardiff
CD4 9XL

Dr Mrs Lander

Following my recent visit to your home here is the estimate for the building and decorating work to be carried out.

Remove dividing ~~adjoining~~ wall to make upstairs toilet and bathroom into one room – £1640

Redecorate master bedroom – £500

Repaint front exterior windows and doors – £350

All our work is guteed and our prices include VAT

All materials, excluding paint, to be supplied by yourself.

We look forward to carrying out this work.

Yours scly

T JONES & SON

EXERCISE 26

Prepare this letter on suitable-sized paper, making the necessary corrections. Type an envelope.

Ref SR/ your initals

Mr S Hemmings   14 Great Croom Hill
Sunderland   SL9 VS3

Dr Mr Hemmings

uc   Your letter has been passed to me by our chief
Executive.

I was sorry to hear that you have had no
response to your telephone calls to our office.
As a company which prides itself on its service
uc   to our customers, i was dismayed to learn
that you have had reason to complain. I
trs   now/can assure you that action has been
taken to supply you with the missing goods
which you should receive within the next
2 days.

I was very pleased to read that you find our
uc   journal Reports so helpful ∧ I am sure you are
correct when you say many students find them
✓   ~~helpful~~ useful.

With regard to storage of the Journals, we
supply a sturdy file in which to keep them. The
file normally costs £5.50 plus VAT, but in view
of yr recent complaint, I am sending you a
complimentary file.

I hope we can continue to be of further
✓   ~~beep~~ assistance in future.

Yrs scly
S Richards

EXERCISE 27

Prepare this A4 letter together with an envelope.

Ref PP/ your initials

RD Taylor 30 Bournside Grove
Liverpool L25 7FD

Dr Sir

1   I am writing to ack recipt of your recent
    letter and apologise for the incon you
run on   have been caused.

Mr Phillips is away on business at
present, but I will pass on your letter
to him when he returns.

printed

(✓) The publication you require is published
    annually in June and it is our policy
    not to sell exciting editions of our
    publications 3 months prior to the new
run on   edition being printed.
    I hope this clarifies the situation.

Yrs ffly

R Green
Secretary to Mr Phillips

EXERCISE 28

Prepare the following draft letter for despatch today.

Mrs R Black 317 George Street London NW2 6TN

Dear Mrs Black

Thank you for yr information request card. We hope you find

NP the enclosed literature on the new style ~~model~~ car of interest. [If

you wd like to test drive this car or if you would like more

details on our other cars, please to not hesitate to contact

us.

Should you be interested in buying a new car from us, and

would like to take advantage of our easy-pay credit facility,

UC Mr Wilson in the credit office will be pleased to advise you.

Yrs scly

G Pritchard
Marketing Manager

Enc

EXERCISE 29

Key in this letter together with an envelope.

Mr T Hilton Univeral House 6 Regency Gardens London W1A 9EJ s/

Dr Mr Hilton

Thanks for your letter wh I recd last week.   run on
I aplogise for the delay in answering but I have just returned
from my holiday. [I would like to confirm that we can meet your NP
requirements by the date agreed and do not fore see any
problems with future delivery dates.

Yrs scly

Janet Montague

EXERCISE 30

Display the following letter on appropriate-sized paper. Type an envelope.

JJ Spoke Ltd
3 Graham Place
Ipswich

Dear Sirs

Last week I collected my watch from your workshop in the Precinct and was told

NP the necy repairs had been carried out. [I have worn the watch everyday since then & not once has it kept the correct time - it gains approx 1½ hrs in every 24.

The repair charge was £11.50 & when I took it back to the shop they refused to help me. Surely your repairs carry some sort of gntee & if not, I feel that something should be done to put my watch right after such a short time.

I look forward to hearing from you.

yrs ffly

Judith Bush

CIRCULAR LETTERS

A circular letter is one which is sent to any number of different people/organisations but which contains the same information. In order to save time typing up the same letter over and over again, circular letters are prepared and printed leaving sufficient space to fill in appropriate details as necessary.

As the letters may be sent out on different occasions, the words 'Date as Postmark' are shown in place of the current date.

Circular letters are prepared using the fully-blocked layout, leaving 9 clear lines between the 'date' and the 'salutation'.

Key in the following sample **circular letter** which shows the correct layout.

Ref Subs/1 *-enter/return twice*

Date as postmark *-enter/return 10 times*

Dear Sir/Madam *-enter/return twice*

We notice that your subscription to the Health and Fitness Club is due for renewal at the end of this month. *-enter/return twice*

In order that we may forward you a current Membership Card would you kindly send in your cheque for £45.00, made payable to the Club and addressed to the Treasurer. *-enter/return twice*

Yours faithfully *-enter/return 6 times*

Club Secretary

EXERCISE 31

Prepare this circular letter on A4 paper. Date it one month from today.

Ref WBL/6

Dear Householder

Want to replace your windows but feel you cannot afford to at the present time?

We have the answer - you can have new windows, doors, patio doors or a conservatory fitted in time for the summer - without using your savings.

With our Loan Plan Scheme your repayments commence three months after the work has been completed. On top of this, we offer a substantial discount and if you place your order within the next three weeks, we will deduct a further 5%.

All our work is guaranteed and is carried out by skilled craftsmen.

CALL NOW FOR A FREE ESTIMATE ON: 0171-486-2195

EXERCISE 32

Prepare this circular letter. Use the correct spacing.

Today's date

Dear Parent/Guardian

Your daughter's Rubella injection is now due.

The School Doctor will be vaccinating the girls in your daughter's class on Tuesday of next week.

Would you please inform us if you are arranging for your own doctor to carry this out.

Yours sincerely

Elizabeth White
School Secretary

EXERCISE 33

Prepare this circular letter with today's date.

Dear Parent/Guardian

As from Monday of next week, builders will be carrying out
extensive repair work on the toilets in the Infant Block.

All the children have been informed and the infants have been
told that they must use the toilets in the Junior Block.

This is bound to cause disruption for a few weeks and we would
ask for your co-operation during the time it takes for the
work to be completed.

It would be of enormous help if, when dropping off and
collecting the children in the morning and afternoon, you
give the building area, which has been "coned off", a wide
berth. Please emphasize to your children that for their own
safety they are not to go anywhere near the area.

We thank you for your help

*Typist – Do not leave 9 lines
for name and address as
this letter will be taken home
by the children.*

Headteacher

EXERCISE 34

Prepare this circular letter leaving sufficient space for figures, where indicated.

Date as postmark

Dear Supersaver

We are pleased to inform you that now your account stands at over £25,000 you qualify for our extra 2% interest. [The amount of £. . . . . . . has been added to your account at our Head Office and in order for this to be shown in your Personal Passbook call in at any of our Branches and present this letter.

Gerald Seymour
Chief Accounts Manager

EXERCISE 35

Prepare this circular letter on A4 paper and date it for despatch tomorrow.

Dear Parent

uc   I see from our records that your child will be starting school next september.

daily h / lc   To help the children settle down we are holding an "open week" the first week of June, from 9-30 - 11-30 am. Your child can visit the school, meet the Teachers n the other children in the class and generally get to know the school building.

NP   In the past, we have found that those children who have come to this "open week" enjoy their first taste of school. [If you find that you are unable to attend, please contact the school secretary on 0181- 355 - 4636.

uc   yours sincerely

Becky Millar
Headteacher

FORM LETTERS

Occasionally letters incorporating a 'tear-off slip' will have to be typed. The fully blocked style is retained throughout as shown on the following example.

Type this example of a form letter on A4 paper.

Ref WW/F1

Today's date

Mr G Evans
20 Kirby Road
Leeds
LS2 6TJ

Dear Mr Evans

Our annual Reunion Dinner is going to be held at The Royal George Hotel for the second year running.

This venue proved to be extremely popular and we have been fortunate to be able to book it again this year.

The Dinner will be held on Saturday 9th November at 7pm and the cost of the tickets this year will be £12 per person.

As this is an extremely popular event, we would ask you to complete and return the tear-off slip within the next few days.

Yours sincerely

George Ashby

....

PLEASE RETURN TO: George Ashby 24 Carlton Crescent Leeds LS3 6TJ

I will/will not* be able to attend the Reunion Dinner on 9th November.

I will/will not* be bringing a guest.

I enclose my cheque for £...................

Signature...

*Delete as applicable.

EXERCISE 36

Key in this circular letter, using double line spacing for the tear-off slip at the bottom of the letter.

Date as postmark

Dear Reader

Thank you for your enquiry about joining our world wide penfriend scheme.

In order that the computer can select a suitable correspondent for you, please fill in your details on the tear-off slip and return it together with the fee of £5.

Yours sincerely

Beverley Sloane

....

Name ....

Address ....

....

....

Postcode ....

Interests/hobbies

....

....

Age of penfriend required .... Male/Female*

Country preferred a)...........................

....

Signature ....

*Please delete as applicable

EXERCISE 37

Prepare this form letter.

Date as postmark

Dear Subscriber
We are currently launching our new Spring brochure. If you introduce a friend who subsequently places an order with us, you will receive a 10% discount voucher redeemable against your next order.

Yours sincerely

Subscription Editor

- -

Name_____ Account no_____

I introduce: Mr/Mrs/Miss/Ms _____

Address_____
_____
Postcode_____

Typist – Tear-off section in double spacing

EXERCISE 38

Make the necessary corrections on this A4 letter.

April (current year)

Dr Member

Ⓥ Our AGM wl be held on 26 May at ~~7·00~~ 7.30 pm

NP at the Clubhouse. [As usual we wl be electing a new cttee ⅄ we would ask you to put forward your nominations on the attached slip.

Yrs scly
Freda Parsons
Club Sec

Nominations —— h/s

a) Chairman ....

b) Vice chairman _ _ _ _ _ _ _ _ _ _ _ _ _

c) Sec ....

uc d) treasurer _ _ _ _ _ _ _ _ _ _ _ _ _ _

e) Club Captain _ _ _ _ _ _ _ _ _ _ _ _

f) Vice Captain _ _ _ _ _ _ _ _ _ _ _ _ _

(typist - this
section in double
line spacing)

CENTRING/DISPLAY

HORIZONTAL CENTRING

This is the term used when work has to be centred across the page, and it is often used for headings.

To achieve this, move the carriage to the middle of the paper, add up the number of characters and spaces to be typed, and then backspace **half** this number.

For example, if using A4 paper, the number of spaces across the top is 100 (elite machines). If the characters, including the spaces, to be centred add up to 20, simply move to the centre of the paper i.e. 50, and backspace **10 spaces**, then type your heading.

If the item to be centred adds up to an odd number, deduct 1 **before** halving the total.

Many machines have an automatic centring facility and the relevant manuals will give specific instructions on how to use it.

On a wordprocessor, use the automatic centring command.

Centre the following example:

A CENTRED HEADING

Centre these exercises:

EXERCISE 1

Your own name (eg Mary Smith)

EXERCISE 2

Your own address (centre each line of the address)

EXERCISE 3

"Centring is easy now"

VERTICAL CENTRING

 You have learnt how to centre your work across the paper; now you must learn how to centre the work down the page. This is known as **vertical centring**.

The example on page 129 is to be typed on A5 landscape paper, which has 100 spaces across the page and 35 lines down the page. Refer to Chapter 4 (General Keyboarding Information), section on paper sizes.

METHOD

1   Add up the number of lines to be typed - including the clear lines, which equals 11 lines.

2   Deduct this amount from 35 (the number of lines on the paper), then divide the answer by 2. This is so that the spacing at the top and bottom are equal.

3   From the top of the paper, turn up 12 lines and add on 1. (This allows for the first line of type.) You are then ready to start the display work.

 If you are using a word processor, change the top and bottom margins from the default setting.

Do not forget to centre the work horizontally. From the centre of the paper backspace half the total of each line.

WELCOME TO OUR HOTEL   35 lines to type on (A5 landscape)

                             −11 lines to type

HEATED SWIMMING POOL   = 24 spare lines to be divided
                             between the top and bottom of

GOOD FAMILY RESTAURANT   the paper. This equals 12.
                             Remember to add on the extra

LUXURY ROOMS   1 before starting to type:
                             i.e. for this exercise turn

REASONABLE PRICES   up 13 **single** lines.

BOOK NOW!

Your finished work should be centred as shown here.

WELCOME TO OUR HOTEL

HEATED SWIMMING POOL

GOOD FAMILY RESTAURANT

LUXURY ROOMS

REASONABLE PRICES

BOOK NOW!

DISPLAY (PRACTICE)

EXERCISE 1

Centre this exercise both vertically and horizontally. Use double line spacing, except where indicated.

ST MARK'S SPRING FAIR

St Mark's Hall   } *Single line spacing*
Wimbledon Road
Northside

Many bargains

Nearly-new stall

Raffle - top prize holiday for two

Saturday 3 April

Doors open 2pm

20p entrance in aid of local charity

Refreshments available

EXERCISE 2

Centre this exercise and keep line spacing as indicated.

Use A5 portrait paper.

Use enhancements i.e. italics, bold, different fonts.

WAXWOODS GARDEN CENTRE

We can supply all your gardening requirements

Trees - Ornamental and fruit

Wide varieties of shrubs and bushes

Special offers on bedding plants

OPEN 7 DAYS A WEEK

Monday - Saturday 0900 - 1800

Sunday - 1000 - 1400

Expert advice always available

Special bulk discount given

ALL ORDERS OVER £75 DELIVERED FREE OF CHARGE

EXERCISE 3

Centre this exercise, using double line spacing.

Use enhancements.

HAZELEA ANNUAL SCHOOL FETE

e⌇ Childrⱨ's Fancy Dress Parade

Bar-B-Que Lunch

Cake Stall

Second Hand Toys

Face Painting

Books and Records

White Elephant Stall

BOUNCY CASTLE

Raffle Prizes - Colour TV 1st Prize

Gates open 11.30

Adults 40p Children/Senior Citizens 10p

BE THERE - DON'T MISS IT

EXERCISE 4

Centre the following exercise. Keep line spacing as shown and make any corrections.

Use enhancements.

THE CIRCUS IS COMING TO TOWN — *underscore heading*

Many Exciting Attractions - including: *t*

Acrobats - Aerial Display - Jugglers
The Amazing Strong man *close up*
Daring Trampoline Display
Fire Eating and Flame Throwing
Magicians and Illusionists

and of course

CLARENCE THE MAGICAL CLOWN

One week only at the Central Stadium

Tickets from £2.50 to £6.00

Performances at 2.30 and 7.30 *transpose*

DON'T MISS THE SHOW

EXERCISE 5

Centre this menu on A4 paper. Follow line spacing as indicated. Type heading in **spaced capitals** (1 space between letters, 3 spaces between words).

P A R K   H O T E L

DINNER MENU

Melon
Avocado Surprise
Chicken Liver Pate

ooOoo

Spring Chicken in Lemon Sauce
Salmon en Croute
Lamb Cutlets

New Potatoes or
Saute Potatoes
French Beans
Baby Carrots

ooOoo

Dutch Apple Pie
Strawberry Pavlova
Trifle

ooOoo

Coffee

EXERCISE 6

Display this advertisement attractively for inclusion in a newspaper.

HOUSEKEEPER/COMPANION REQUIRED

Elderly lady needs companion

Duties to include:

Light housework and cooking

Transportation to local day centre

Occasional trips to concert/theatre

Car driver/non-smoker essential
References required
Salary negotiable

Apply to Box no 826

EXERCISE 7

Display this exercise attractively using suitable-sized paper.

PIANO FOR SALE

Beautiful Victorian Piano

Excellent Condition

lc Regularly Tuned

lc Will Deliver if Necessary

£120
Ring 01732-88-1627 after 6.00pm

EXERCISE 8

Type the following notice for display on the school notice board. Make your own line spacing and centre every line.

CAREERS ADVICE

Friday 8 May
Room 12 at 11.00 am with:
Ms Jill Hamett — Careers Officer
Advice given on the following:-
Further/Higher Education
Banking
Nursing
Teaching
Law
Accountancy
Design

See your form tutor for further details.

EXERCISE 9

Prepare the following notice, centring both horizontally and vertically.

St John's Scouts

CAR BOOT SALE — (Spaced Caps)

Saturday 30 June
1·00 — 3.30 pm

Scout Hut Car Park

Cars £5·00   Vans £6·00
Admission 25p   ) trs

Contact G Hill Tel. No. 0181-882-3151

EXERCISE 10

Display this recipe following the line spacing indicated.

Yoghurt Cake   — *Caps and underscore*

1 pot plain yoghurt
3 pots s.r. flour
2 pots caster sugar
3 eggs
1 pot oil
a few drops vanilla essence
3 tspns baking powder
chopped fruit - apple, pear etc. (optional)

e/   Blend all the ingredients together, pour into a large, lightly
NP greased ring mould. [Bake in a moderate oven, gas mark 4 for
30-40 minutes.

delicious! — *Caps*

EXERCISE 11

 Display the following notice. Use line spacing, underscoring, blocked capitals and spaced capitals effectively.

 Use any enhancements available on your PC.

JUNIOR TALENT COMPETITION

Auditions to be held
on
Saturday 10 May
1000-1830
Town Hall - (Turner Room)
High Road
Cheltenham
We are looking for children with the following talents
Musicians
Dancers
Singers
Magicians
Gymnasts
Band/Pop groups
Impressionists
Age groups: 5-8, 9-12
For further details and an application form, contact:
Adrian Cooper on 0163-7932 ext 54
Application forms to be submitted by end March

EXERCISE 12

Set margins at 10 and 60.

ST BARTHOLOMEW'S COLLEGE — *Centre and underscore*

During the months of July and August, we are pleased to announce that the following short courses will be available.

Calligraphy
Pottery
Cake decoration
Aromatherapy
Mixed crafts   *Centre each line*
Jewellery making
Water colours for beginners
Yoga
Interior design
Picture framing

Times and prices of the courses will vary. For further details write to

Judy Reynolds
St Bartholomew's College   ← *Type at left hand margin*
Short Course Unit
Middleton Road
Brighton
Sussex
or telephone Brighton 4920

FULLY BLOCKED CENTRING

As an alternative to centring every line horizontally, the fully blocked method can be used. This is much quicker as only the longest line is centred.

 In the following example, the longest line only is counted and once you have backspaced half the total from the centre, the left-hand margin is set. All remaining lines then start from this point.

 Change the margins to centre the longest line, and keep the ragged right margin.

SOPHIE'S FLOWER SHOP

Floral Displays for all Occasions

Engagements and Weddings
Christenings
Anniversaries
Births
Funerals

Dried flower displays available to order *(longest line)*

EXERCISE 13

Using the fully blocked method of centring, display this exercise.

WATERWORLD INDOOR FUN PARK

An exciting day out for all the family

Swimming pool/wave machine
Theme pool
Fabulous water chutes
Ride the Rapids
Lazy river ride
Kiddies Korner

Beautiful tropical surroundings

Relax in our Safari bar/restaurant

EXERCISE 14

Set this menu out using the fully blocked method of centring.

THE ROYAL HERITAGE HOTEL

Luncheon Menu

Midweek Special £8.95

Fruit Juice
Soup of the Day
Duck Paté

--O--

Lamb Chops in Wine Sauce
Braised Kidneys
Chicken Marengo
Vegetable Lasagne

Roast, Boiled, Saute Potatoes
Green Beans
Cauliflower

--O--

Peach Melba
Apple Pie
Ice Cream - Assorted Flavours

--O--

Coffee

EXERCISE 15

Using the fully blocked centring method, display the following.

THE WESTSIDE ARENA

Presents

A Charity Concert
In Aid of Save the Environment

June 22 at 7.30pm

Featuring top names in popular entertainment

Guest appearances throughout the evening

Tickets from the box office only

MEMORANDA

A memorandum is a written message sent through an Internal Mail System to people working for the same organisation.

A memorandum does not require any formal salutation or complimentary close as used on letters.

Many organisations these days have pre-printed memorandum sheets and the relevant details need only be filled in. However if a printed sheet is not available, use the fully blocked layout. The instructions and an example are shown below.

1   If using A5 paper, have the wider edge at the top. Set margins at 18 and 72. Turn down 5 lines from the top. Type MEMORANDUM at the margin. Then press enter/return twice.

2   The section showing where the memo has originated from and where it is going to, together with the date and reference (if given) is always typed in double line spacing.

3   Return/enter twice before typing the SUBJECT. (Not all memos have a subject heading.)

4   Return/enter twice and type the information.

EXAMPLE

MEMORANDUM

TO   Sales Manager   *(enter/return twice)*

FROM   Managing Director   *(enter/return twice)*

REF   RW/LW   *(enter/return twice)*

DATE   (today's date)   *(enter/return twice)*

SUBJECT Memo writing   *(enter/return twice)*

When writing or typing memoranda, remember that you do not
need to type in a name and address. All that is needed is the
name or title of the sender and recipient of the memo.
Occasionally the department may be shown.

Key in the following exercises using A5 paper unless otherwise indicated.

EXERCISE 1

MEMORANDUM

TO   All Typing Students

FROM   Course Tutor

DATE   (Today's)

SUBJECT Typing Assessment

In order to pass the initial typing assessment, it is imperative that you are able to type a passage of approximately 250 words with 95% accuracy. You must also be able to prepare a letter and a memorandum using the fully blocked style.

EXERCISE 2

MEMORANDUM

TO   ALL STAFF

FROM   PERSONNEL DEPT

DATE   (Today's)

REF   PD/H

CANTEEN OPENING

The catering department are pleased to announce that now the
modernisation work is completed, the canteen will be open
from 11.30 to 2.30 for lunches as well as snacks, as from next
Monday.

The improvement to the kitchen will mean a greater variety
of meals will be available for all employees. There will,
however, be no increase in the cost of the lunches for the
time being.

EXERCISE 3

MEMORANDUM

TO   Mr Hills - Transport Manager

FROM Salaries Department

DATE (Today's)

REF   S/2

Will you please inform all your weekly paid staff that their salary cheques can now be collected after 3.00 pm on Thursdays or Fridays, as from next week.

EXERCISE 4

Prepare this longer memo on A4 paper.

MEMORANDUM

TO   All Course Tutors

FROM   Head of Department

DATE   (Today's)

SUBJECT   Examination Entries

Please ensure that all students wishing to enter for the summer series of external examinations have completed and submitted their application forms before the Easter break. The forms must be authorised by both the Course Tutor and the Head of Department.

Impress on your students that forms received after the Easter holidays will not be accepted under any circumstances.

Payment for all examinations must be made through the Finance Office which is open every day between 10.00 and 3.00.

Attached is a list giving details of the relevant examination entry fees. Please note that this year, students who were under 18 when they joined the course will have a 25% reduction in the fees. They will, however, still have to pay the full administration charge.

Examination application forms are available from Frances in the general office.

EXERCISE 5

Prepare this memo from the Sales Director to the Catering Department.
Date it today and give it the subject heading 'Japanese Visitors'.

As you know we are expecting a group of Japanese businessmen
to visit our new factory and warehouse on Tuesday of next week.

They will be spending the whole day with us and will,
therefore, require morning coffee, luncheon and afternoon
tea. All refreshments will be taken in the Directors' Dining
Room.

They have specifically requested that they be served typical
English fare for their luncheon. Perhaps you would let me
have a few sample menus to choose from.

EXERCISE 6

Type this memo, making the necessary corrections.

To Debbie, From Stephanie. Subject - Summer Collection

Here are the fabric samples for our range of beach culottes.
I particularly like the lemon and mauve wh wl team up well
with the T-shirts you are working on.

May we get together for a meeting on Tues next week to finalise
those items to be included in the next cat. Ring me if this is
not convenient.

EXERCISE 7

```
TO     ERIC LLEWELLYN
FROM   CLAIRE WOODS
REF    SA/2
```

Further to your note and our subsequent telephone
uc conversation, I can see no objection to Mr ortega continuing
N.P as our agent in South America. [He has done extremely well
over the last year in spite of local difficulties, & I feel he
should continue to expand the business.

EXERCISE 8

To The Principal

From Business Studies Dept

Date

Margaret Barrett's Retirement

We have had a collection for Margaret's
leaving present ∧ have bought her a
NP garden table and 4 chairs. [We hope
you will be able to present this gift
to her next Wed evening at 7.30pm,
at her "surprise" leaving party.

EXERCISE 9

This memo is to go to All Staff from the Personnel Manager. The subject is Car Parking.

In order to park in the staff car park, will you please display on your windscreen a Company Parking Sticker. These are obtainable from Miss Goff in the Personnel Department.

Visitors should be advised that they will need to call in at Reception where they will be given a Visitors Parking Sticker for display on their windscreen.

It is hoped that this scheme will discourage non-employees from using our parking facilities.

EXERCISE 10

Memo
To: All Reps
From: Sales Director
Subject: Sales Figures

May I please have your sales figures for the months Jan, Feb and March on my
NP desk by Tues of next week. [These are
uc urgently required for the Board meeting
on Thurs.

EXERCISE 11

Type this memo to the Typing Supervisor from Miss G Atherton. The subject is Stationery Supplies.

It has been brought to my notice that over the past few months our stationery supplies have been rapidly diminishing. We have decided to introduce a complete ✓ system whereby all staff must sign a Request Form, to be signed by either myself or the Personnel NP Officer, in order to obtain supplies. [Please inform members of staff in your Dept of this new procedure.

EXERCISE 12

Memorandum

To   The Transport Manager

trs   From Accounts   Miss Gresham

Date   Today's

Could you ask all Reps to let me have a note of their mileage by the end of this week.

Please remind them that petrol expense forms must be submitted to this office by the last Wed of every month so that payment can be made promptly.

EXERCISE 13

MEMORANDUM

To Brian Major — Works Manager
                             Cheltenham
From Hilary Lewis - Personnel
                             London

Mr David Green will be joining our
Management Team as from next month.
It is our intention that, during his
first weeks with us, he visits all our
uc *factories* and meets the Managers and
NP staff. [He is due to collect his company
car from the suppliers in Cheltenham
on the Wed of his first week. Could
you therefore meet him from the
7 o'clock train on that day, give him
a guided tour of the factory and
introduce him to your staff?

are∧ If there ∧ any problems with this
arrangement please let me know as
soon as poss.

EXERCISE 14

Memorandum

To Pool Manager
From Manager Leisure Services

Date Today's

Subject Towels

We have now received our delivery
of the new range of towels.

uc As you requested, those for use in the
Pool area are in aqua shades & those
for use in the Sauna are in Peach.

Please ask your staff to see that
they do not get mixed up.

TABULATION

Tabulation is the typing of information in evenly spaced columns. Tabulation is an extension of centring/display work. Work can either be ruled or boxed, or simply set out without any ruling up.

The following example shows how to work out and set out ordinary tabulation.

```
BREAD       MILK        PEARS
CAKE        CHEESE      PEACHES
BISCUITS    YOGHURTS    APPLES
POTATOES    CHOCOLATE   ORANGES
```

1 Calculate the vertical centring (see section on Centring/Display) for the above example which is in single line spacing, using A5 landscape paper; i.e. turn up 16 single lines.

2 Add up the number of characters in the longest line in each column.

    e.g. POTATOES   = 8
          CHOCOLATE = 9
          PEACHES   = 7

3 Leave 5 spaces between each of the columns.

4 Add ALL the figures together: 8 + 5 + 9 + 5 + 7 = 34.

5 From the centre of your paper, backspace half of this total, i.e. 17 spaces. At this point SET YOUR LEFT-HAND MARGIN.

6 Before setting your tab stops, be sure to delete any existing tab stops by using the TAB CLEAR FACILITY.

7   From the left-hand margin, using the space bar, tap in the width of the first column (8) plus the space (5) which will bring you to the second column, at which point **set a tab**. Tap in the width of this second column (9) plus the space (5) and set the second tab for the third column.

8   The machine will then automatically stop at these points when you press the **tab key**. Do this for each column.

At tab menu, clear the existing default tabs and reset them as in instruction 7.

Type the following exercises, making sure that they are centred vertically and horizontally.

EXERCISE 1

Use A5 landscape paper and double line spacing.

COUNTRY	CAPITAL	LANGUAGE
Italy	Rome	Italian
England	London	English
Spain	Madrid	Spanish
France	Paris	French
Sweden	Stockholm	Swedish

EXERCISE 2

Turn up 3 lines after typing the heading and then type the rest in double
line spacing.

Use A5 landscape paper.

```
CATS        DOGS        BIRDS       FISH

Manx        Labrador    Sparrow     Salmon
Siamese     Spaniel     Blackbird   Dover Sole
Tabby       Terrier     Thrush      Plaice
Persian     Poodle      Starling    Haddock
```

EXERCISE 3

Key in the following exercise keeping spacing as shown.

Use A5 landscape paper.

HOLIDAY LIST — *Spaced caps and underscore*

```
skirts      shirts          shorts       sandals

camera      washing items   sunglasses   towel

book        money           passport     first aid kit

beachwear   tissues         sun oil      beach bag
```

EXERCISE 4

Prepare this in double line spacing. Leave 3 spaces between the columns.

AIRLINES AND THEIR EMBLEMS

BA	British Airways	UK
TWA	Trans World Airlines	USA
SAS	Scandinavian Airlines	SCANDINAVIA
ALITALIA	Italian Airlines	ITALY
SABENA	Belgium Airlines	BELGIUM
PAN AM	Pan American	USA
QANTAS	Australian Airlines	AUSTRALIA
JAL	Japanese Airlines	JAPAN
KLM	Royal Dutch Airlines	HOLLAND
SAA	South African Airways	SOUTH AFRICA

EXERCISE 5

Prepare this list. Keep layout as shown.

Wedding Anniversaries

First	Paper	Thirteenth	Lace
Second	Calico	Fourteenth	Ivory
Third	Leather	Fifteenth	Crystal
Fourth	Silk	Twentieth	China
Fifth	Wood	Twenty-fifth	Silver
Sixth	Iron	Thirtieth	Pearl
Seventh	Copper	Thirty-fifth	Coral or Jade
Eighth	Bronze	Fortieth	Ruby
Ninth	Pottery	Forty-fifth	Golden
Tenth	Tin	Fiftieth	Sapphire
Eleventh	Steel	Fifty-fifth	Emerald
Twelfth	Linen	Sixtieth	Diamond

EXERCISE 6

Use A5 paper.

Turn up 3 lines after the heading. Type the rest in single line spacing.

Subjects for Examination   (caps and centre)

Accounts	Cookery	History	Russian*
Arithmetic	English	Housecraft	Science
Art	Economics	Italian*	Shorthand
Biology	French*	Mechanics	Spanish*
Chemistry	Finnish*	Music	Statistics
Classics	Geography	Needlecraft	Typewriting
Commerce	German*	Physics	Woodwork

* Language Exams in two parts: written and oral.

EXERCISE 7

Use A5 landscape paper for this exercise.

The Stationery Cupboard   u/s Heading

A4 Paper	Envelopes	Stapler	Pens
Carbon ,,	Postcards	Staples	Pencils
Flimsy ,,	Labels	Paper clips	Erasers
Headed ,,	Sellotape	Scissors	Rulers

Typist — do not use ditto marks

EXERCISE 8

Use A5 portrait paper.

SPORTS DAY — spaced caps

Column heading in capitals

Event	Time	Starter
100 yds sprint	10.00	Mr Woods
400 yds hurdle	11.30	Mr Dodman
Javelin	11.00	Mrs Goddard
High Jump	10.15	Miss Sullivan
Long Jump	11.45	Mr Jones
Marathon	12.00	Mr Singh

trs times only

Competitors must report to the starter at least 5 minutes before event is due to start.

EXERCISE 9

Use suitable-sized paper and prepare in double line spacing.

<u>HERBS & SPICES</u>

Aniseed	Garlic	Bay	Parsley
Dill	Basil	Paprika	Rosemary
Nutmeg	Cumin	Thyme	Sage
Saffron	Caraway	Cloves	Allspice
Tarragon	Oregano	Mustard	Mace

Typist – rearrange this list in to alphabetical order. Keep to four columns

EXERCISE 10

Key in using double line spacing.

Before starting the exercise, refer to the section 'Typing Figures' in Chapter 4 (General Keyboarding Information).

AUCTION PRICE LIST

Lot No	Item	Reserve Price
		£
463	Nest of tables	165.00
129	Pearl necklace	240.00
43	Pine bookcase	65.75
5	Tea set (complete)	25.00
28	Upright piano	185.50
261	Silver candlesticks	95.75
563	Gentleman's gold fob watch	375.00
564	Lady's gold dress watch	550.00
42	Framed oil painting	55.45
76	Mahogany desk	175.00
94	6 dining chairs	120.00
8	Dining table (to match lot 94)	80.00
184	Edwardian overmantle	285.00
32	Victorian washstand	145.00
631	Persian carpet	72.00
2	Pine wardrobe	130.00
7	Silver/enamel brooch	22.65
89	Canteen of cutlery	196.00

PLEASE NOTE THAT ALL ITEMS MUST BE PAID FOR IN FULL BEFORE BEING COLLECTED.

EXERCISE 11

Type on A5 landscape paper.

Centre main heading.

WAXWOODS BEAUTY CLINIC — spaced caps
PRICE LIST — uls

Treatment	Single Session	Course of 6
	£	£
Facial	9·00	50·00
Leg waxing from	12·50	N/A
Eyelash tinting	3·00	16·00
Manicure	4·75	23·25
Pedicure	"	"
Aromatherapy	16·00	22·50
Sun bed	4·00	80·00
Electrolysis from	3·75	Prices vary

Typist – do not use ditto marks.

EXERCISE 12

Type on A5 portrait paper.

Phonetic Alphabet — CAP & u/s

A = Alpha   N = November
B = Bravo   O = Oscar
C = Charlie   P = Papa
D = Delta   Q = Quebec
E = Echo   R = Romeo
F = Foxtrot   S = Sierra
G = Golf   T = Tango
H = Hotel   U = Uniform
I = India   V = Victor
J = Juliet   W = Whiskey
K = Kilo   X = X-ray
L = Lima   Y = Yankee
M = Mike   Z = Zulu

BOXED OR RULED TABULATION

Boxed or **ruled** tabulation is an extension of ordinary tabulation. The basic rules must be followed; the only difference is that spacing must be allowed for ruling up.

It is important to remember that all horizontal lines are typed in, only the vertical lines are drawn in afterwards. You may use either a sharp pointed pencil or black pen for these lines. Felt tips are not suitable.

This example shows you how to work out your tabulation and rule it up.

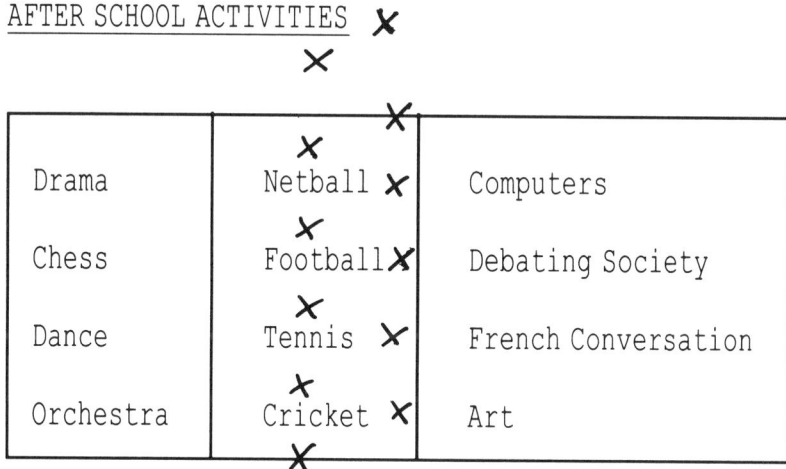

1   When calculating the **vertical** centring include the horizontal lines and the space underneath. This example uses 12 lines - the crosses show each line.

2   Follow the instructions for basic tabulation numbers 2–6.

Now continue:

7   From the left-hand margin tap in the width of the first column (9) plus the space (5) and set a tab. Tap in the width of the second column (8) plus the space (5) and set a tab. Tap in the width **only** of the third column (19) and set the right-hand margin.

8   After typing the heading return the carriage twice ready to type the horizontal line. This line extends 2 spaces either side of the type to create an even border.

9   At the left-hand margin, using the **margin release key**, backspace twice and begin to type in the line using the underscore. At the right-hand margin, press the **margin release key** and type two more lines.

10 In **double** line spacing type the text. Return to **single** line spacing before typing the bottom horizontal line - follow the instructions given in 9 above.

11 To rule up the **vertical** lines, go to the first tab stop and backspace 3 spaces (this is the centre of the two columns). Make a light pencil mark below the top line. Repeat this at the second tab stop. At the bottom of the exercise do the same but make the pencil mark above the line. Remove the work and rule it up carefully.

Use your table facility to complete the following exercises.

Use A5 paper in exercises 1–10 unless otherwise indicated.

EXERCISE 1

Following the instructions of ruled tabulation, type up this exercise in double line spacing.

<u>DECORATING MATERIALS</u>

Wallpaper	Paint	Ladder
Paste	Brushes	Dust sheets
Scissors	Stencils	Bucket
Plumbline	Sponge	Scaffolding

EXERCISE 2

Rule as indicated, and make necessary corrections.

RECEPTION DUTY

Lunch-time cover

Name	Day	Time
Felicity Jones	Monday	12.00 – 2.00
Grace Allen	Tues "	11.30 – 1.30
John Wickford	Wed "	12.00 – 2.00
Mary Ward	Thurs	12.30 – 2.30
David Adams	Fri	11.30 – 1.30

trs columns

Type days in full

EXERCISE 3

EXAM RESULTS

Name	Shorthand	Typing	W.P
Angela Staines	Pass	Pass*	Pass
Helena Carpenter	Fail	Pass	Pass
Michelle Jones	Fail	Pass	Pass
Laura Harvey	Pass	Pass*	Pass*
Carol Farley	Pass*	Pass	Fail
Paul Garrard	Pass	Pass	Pass

*Denotes Distinction

EXERCISE 4

Sales Turnover	1989 £	1990 £
London	21, 849	25, 326
Midlands	16, 732	18, 641
West Country	15, 716	15, 819
Scotland	26, 321	28, 969
Wales	19, 356	21,004

EXERCISE 5

Paint	Wallpaper	Fabric
Cream	Orchard View	Orchard Meadow
Rose	Garden Scene	Apple Patch
Sand	Desert Sand	Desert Sun
Peach	Peach Trellis	Silky Peach

EXERCISE 6

Popular Wines / Liqueurs — caps

Red Wine	White Wine	Liqueur
Beaujolais	Champagne	Port
Burgundy	Sauternes	Brandy
Medoc	Muscadet	Cointreau
Chianti	Chablis	Drambuie
Rioja	Moselle	Grand Marnier

EXERCISE 7

Clematis	Fuchsia	Prunus	Spiraea
Laburnum	Daphne	Lilac	Potentilla
Hydrangea	Passion Flower	Wisteria	Mulberry
Buddleia	Holly Ivy	Japonica	Jasmine
Rosa	Rhododendron	Heather	Forsythia
Pyracantha	Willow	Elder	Camellia

EXERCISE 8

Wages Deduction Sheet — caps and us

Name	Gross Pay this week	Gross Pay this year	Income Tax this week	National Insurance Contribution
James Brown	£156.25	£3934.25	£19.14	£12.26
Alex Ford	£120.01	£3720.00	£21.75*	£10.32
Francis Baker	£148.88	£4386.30	£29.87	£13.39

* Tax coding to be confirmed.

EXERCISE 9

Display effectively, ruling as shown.

JUNIOR ORCHESTRA PLAYERS — u/s

Name	Instrument	Tutor
Judith Jackson	Saxophone	G Levy
Katie Manning	Flute	M White
Laura Carter	Recorder	J Davis
Claire Goddard	Piano	J Davis
Gary Duke	Guitar	A Yeats
Jane Kingsley	Violin	A Yeats
Stephen Woods	Clarinet	M White

EXERCISE 10

Oven temperatures — centre & caps.

	Degrees Celsius	Degrees Fahrenheit	Gas Mark	
				single line spacing
Very cool	110 120	225 250	$\frac{1}{4}$ $\frac{1}{2}$	single line spacing
Cool or slow	140 150	275 300	1 2	single line spacing
Warm	160	325	3	
Moderately hot	190	375	5	
Moderate	180	350	4	
Fairly hot	200	400	6	
Hot	220	425	7	
Very hot	230 240	450 475	8 9	single line spacing

FORMS

The preparation and completion of forms is a necessary skill and is often included in examinations. They are not difficult but it is important to follow the guidelines outlined below.

1   When preparing forms, it is essential to use double line spacing to enable the relevant details to be typed in. At least one space must be left between the 'type' and the dotted line.

2   Make sure that you do not type on the dotted lines, you should be slightly above them. Half a line space is considered to be acceptable.

3   Start three spaces in from the first dot.

4   Typing should not extend beyond the last dot.

5   When deleting, line up the carriage with the word/s to be deleted, using the small 'x' to cover the word/s.

EXAMPLE

Name ....Mr Andrew MacGregor.............   CORRECT VERSION

Address .....24 Stewart Road....................   Too high

Post town ..Edinburgh.....................   Too low

Telephone number .....Edinburgh 8693429.....   Paper not straight

 Prepare forms as instructed and complete either by hand or on a typewriter.

Before attempting the exercises type some dotted lines, in double line spacing, and practise typing your own name and address.

Use the **half-line space key** or the **interliner** to help you find the correct position.

EXERCISE 1

Type this exercise on A5 landscape paper. Re-insert and type in the details given.

DENTAL APPOINTMENT CARD

Name .... *Joyce Mitchell* ....

Clinic Reference No .... **53681/R** ....

Date of Appointment ...... **29/10/93** ....

Time .... **2.30p.m.** ....

Next Appointment ....

EXERCISE 2

Prepare this exercise twice using the particulars given under 'A' and then 'B'.

NAME   ....

ADDRESS   ....

              ....

POST CODE ....

TELEPHONE
NUMBER   ....

Details for 'A':   'B':

Susan Winslow   Mr A Cristofi
66 Belgrave Gardens   95 Park Square
Portsmouth   Ponders End
PT56 6MT   EN1 6BR

Portsmouth 34078   0181-804-9623

EXERCISE 3

Prepare this enrolment form and complete with the details given.

ENROLMENT FORM — East Ridings College

Name ..PHILLIP..WOODMAN.. (CAPS)

Address 19..The..Terrace...........................

York..YK3..IRN.........................

Class Code Number .B604.... Day ...Tuesday........

Class Title Picture Framing. Time ...7.30 — 9.30...

I agree to abide by the college rules, and to pay the fees by the due date.

Signature .... Date ..Today's....

EXERCISE 4

Prepare and complete the following.

Library Book Request Form — (caps and underscore)

Please reserve the following :—

Title ....

Author ....

Publisher..

Own name / address ....

....

....

....

Membership No ....

Details to be filled in :— "Travelling around France" by Marcel Dumenil. Publisher is not known. Requested by Eileen Browne, 84 The Ride, Bexley, Kent. Membership No EB641

EXERCISE 5

Key in this exercise twice in double line spacing. Fill in the details given in Message 1 and Message 2.

TELEPHONE MESSAGE

Date .... Time ....
To .... From ....
Message ....
....
....
....
....

Received
by ....

Message 1:

To Mr Johnson from the Catering Manager. The message was taken at 11.30am.

Mr Greig rang. He is unable to obtain replacement dishes from the original supplier by the time required.

Will you phone him before 4 pm today.

(Type your own name at the 'Received by' line.)

Message 2:

To Pauline Brown from Julie Edwards – Advertising. Can Pauline find out the date and time of the meeting at which the presentation will be made to Bill on his retirement?

Julie rang at 2.30pm.

(Type your own name at the 'Received by' line.)

CURRICULUM VITAE (CV)

A CV is a summary of personal details, education and work experience.

As the CV is likely to be the "first impression" of you, it is important that the data is presented in a logical and concise manner. All relevant information should be included together with any additional items that may be of interest.

It should be noted that all information is usually given in chronological order, with the most recent listed first.

An example of a skeleton CV is given below:

CURRICULUM VITAE
NAME
ADDRESS
TELEPHONE
DATE OF BIRTH   **AGE**
EDUCATION
QUALIFICATIONS
FURTHER EDUCATION
QUALIFICATIONS
WORK EXPERIENCE
HOBBIES/INTERESTS
PERSONAL STATEMENT
REFERENCES

EXERCISE 1

Key in this example of a completed CV.

CURRICULUM VITAE

NAME	Robert Tarrant
ADDRESS	67 Southern Avenue Dartford Kent DA1 4JU
TELEPHONE	01736-942181
DATE OF BIRTH	10 March 1972 **AGE** 23 years old
EDUCATION	Dartford High, London Road, Dartford

QUALIFICATIONS	GCSE: English (language/ literature), Maths, German, Geography, Art
FURTHER EDUCATION	South London College of Further Education
QUALIFICATIONS	GNVQ LEVEL III – Business Studies (includes Word Processing (Windows) Database, Spreadsheets)
WORK EXPERIENCE	Carstairs Catering Hire (1990 to present time) Office Clerk dealing with customers and related documentation. Duties include bookkeeping and daily organisation of the hiring and collection of goods. Promoted to Office Manager after 30 months with 6 office staff.
HOBBIES/INTERESTS	Playing football for a local team on Sunday. Amateur Dramatics and photography.
PERSONAL STATEMENT	I am a fit and healthy person who enjoys meeting and working with the public. I am ambitious and hardworking and would like to broaden my career by taking on a more challenging position. I own a car and have a clean driving licence.
REFERENCES	Mrs J Haversham, Carstairs Catering Hire, Petersham Road, Dartford, Kent.

ITINERARY

An itinerary is a travel plan which can include the following:

dates, times, addresses, telephone numbers, contacts, travel arrangements and any other relevant information.

The distribution of an itinerary may be as under:

1   The person to whom the details apply.

2   The Secretary/Assistant to the above.

3   File copy.

EXERCISE 1

Key in this example of a typical itinerary.

ITINERARY
for Sue Richardson's visit to Artamon Hotel, Coventry
21–23 March

21 March	0800 hrs	Train from Kings Cross
	1015 hrs	Arrive Coventry to be met by David Wentworth. Check in to Hotel
	1100 hrs	Area Sales Meeting (Northern Reps)
	1300 hrs	Lunch at Artamon Hotel, Coventry
	1430 hrs	Area Sales Meeting (Southern Reps)
	1630 hrs	Afternoon tea and summing up.
	2030 hrs	Dinner with David Wentworth, Simon Charles, Caroline Beaumont and Julia Smythe at The Pacific Garden Restaurant.
22 March	0900 hrs	Presentation by the Johnston Consultancy Agency on "Technology in the 21st Century"
	1100 hrs	Coffee
	1130 hrs	Question and Answer Session on above.
	1300 hrs	Lunch (buffet style)
	1430 hrs	Brainstorming session with all Reps.
	1630 hrs	Afternoon tea and summing up.
	2000 hrs	Dinner with Thomas Roydon, Sanjit Shah, Daphne Bradwell.
23 March	1030 hrs	Train from Coventry.
	1245 hrs	Arrive Kings Cross. Take taxi back to Office
	1430 hrs	Deliver preliminary report on above visit.

EXERCISE 2

Key in the following exercise as shown.

TRAVEL ITINERARY – MONDAY 8 OCTOBER

Depart	Arrive	Details
0915 hrs	1100 hrs	London to Leicester by train
	1115 hrs	Taxi to Miller's Wholesalers 12 High Street Tel: 01532-78614
1400 hrs	1530 hrs	Train to Nottingham – Meet Judith Simkins 55 Merchant Place Tel: 01732-884561
1730 hrs	1800 hrs	Westside Hotel Short Street Tel: 01732-874520
1900 hrs	1930 hrs	Dinner at Plaza Hotel with Andrew Green – Bakers' Federation

MEETINGS

Most businesses will hold their meetings on a regular basis.

Before a meeting takes place a **notice of meeting** is sent to those invited to attend. This indicates the date, time and place.

Details of items to be discussed at the meeting are sent out as an **agenda**. This is set out in a specific order and acts as a programme of the meeting.

At the meeting **minutes** are taken of all points discussed.

Key in the following examples of the above documents.

EXERCISE 1

NOTICE OF MEETING

You are invited to attend the next meeting of the Social Committee to be held at the Club House on Thursday 24th May at 7.30pm.

Please advise if you are unable to attend.

Social Secretary
10th May

EXERCISE 2

AGENDA

1. Apologies for absence.

2. Minutes of the last meeting.

3. Matters arising.

4. Correspondence.

5. Reports from: Treasurer
                    Membership Secretary
                    Club Captain

6. Subscriptions.

7. New Members.

8. Any other business.

9. Date of next meeting.

EXERCISE 3

MINUTES

Minutes of Sports Club Meeting held on 24th May at 7.30pm in the Clubhouse.

ACTION

1. APOLOGIES FOR ABSENCE
   A Pullen, L Williamson and S de Lange

2. MINUTES of the last meeting were read and approved.

3. MATTERS ARISING
   The resurfacing of the tennis courts will commence during the first week
   in October. Peter Bruce has agreed to supervise the work.   PB

4. CORRESPONDENCE
   Our allocation for tickets for Wimbledon has now been received. The usual draw
   will be held in due course.

5. REPORTS
   Treasurer – A profit of £157.62 was made at the recent Quiz Evening.
   Thanks to all who participated.

   Membership Secretary – A current list of all members is now posted on
   the Notice Board.

   Club Captain – Nothing to report.

6. SUBSCRIPTIONS
   All subscriptions for the current year have now been received.
   The discount offered for prompt payment has obviously had a good effect.

7. NEW MEMBERS
   An advertisement for the Open Day is to be placed in the local paper next week.
   This should attract several new members.   DS

8. ANY OTHER BUSINESS
   Cathy Hughes gave birth to a baby boy last Tuesday. Flowers and a card
   are to be sent from the Club.   LW

9. DATE OF NEXT MEETING
   23rd July at the Clubhouse, 7.30pm.

Chapter **4**
General Keyboarding Information

PERSONAL COMPETENCY CHECKLIST

Skill	Acquired
Accurate touch typing	
Paragraphs • blocked	
• indented	
• hanging	
Headings	
Correction signs	
Manuscript typing	
Word division	
Common abbreviations	
Proof reading	
Paper sizes	
Letters • Business	
• Circular	
• Form	
Envelopes	
Display/centring • vertical	
• horizontal	
Memoranda	
Tabulation	
Ruled tabulation/Tables	
Forms - preparation	
completion	
Curriculum Vitae	
Itineraries	
Meetings	

PAPER SIZES

Spaces across width of paper:

A4 (210 x 297 mm) - portrait-   100 spaces (12 pitch)
                                                   80 spaces (10 pitch)

A5 (210 x 148 mm) - landscape - 100 spaces (12 pitch)
                                                   80 spaces (10 pitch)

A5 (148 x 210 mm) - portrait -   70 spaces (12 pitch)
                                                   60 spaces (10 pitch)

Number of single line spaces down the page:

A4 - portrait -   70 lines

A5 - landscape - 35 lines

A5 - portrait -   50 lines

Half A4 is A5
Half A5 is A6

```
12 pitch - 100 spaces
10 pitch -  80 spaces

        A5
     Landscape

   35 lines down
```

```
10 pitch -  80 spaces
12 pitch - 100 spaces
        A4
      Portrait




70 lines down
```

```
12 pitch - 70 spaces
10 pitch - 60 spaces


        A5
      Portrait


   50 lines down
```

PRINTERS'/MANUSCRIPT CORRECTION SIGNS

Symbol shown in margin	*Meaning*	*Symbol shown in text*	*Meaning*
l.c.	lower case (small letters)	A̲	under letter/letters to be altered
uc	Upper case (capital letters)	a̲	under letter/letters to be altered
NP	new paragraph	// or ⌐	indicates beginning of new paragraph
run on	no new paragraph	⌐	continue typing on same line
stet ✓	type word/s with dotted lines underneath	home ~~house~~	under the word/s crossed out
∧ a	insert letter, word/s indicated	∧	placed where omission has occurred
∂	delete	the ~~the~~ or. hou∕se	indicates letter/word to be deleted
#	insert space	∧	indicates where space is required
I-I	insert hyphen	∧	indicates where hyphen is required
⌒	close up	clo⌒se	shown between letters/words
trs	transpose (change order **of** letters or words as indicated)	te∫h	between letters or words. Sometimes numbered
us	underline/ underscore	‾	under characters to be underlined
⌐SPELL⌐	clarifies spelling (do not type in capitals unless instructed)	(spell)	word highlighted
CAPS or. ═	type in capitals	‾	words underlined
═ us	type in capitals and underline	‾	words underlined
≡	type in spaced capitals Do not underline unless instructed	‾	words underlined

USE OF CARBON PAPER

In most modern offices copies of any work produced can be taken on photo-copying machines. However, it is necessary to understand and be competent in the use of carbon as it is a requirement of several of the Examining Boards.

How to use carbon paper

1   Place the carbon paper between two sheets of paper, ensuring that the carbonised side faces down onto the second sheet.
2   Keeping the papers together, insert them into the machine, with the carbonised side facing you. As they are fed round the platen, the carbonised side will be away from you.

Type this exercise with a carbon copy:

When using carbon paper, it is important to ensure that you put the carbon paper in the correct way round. Before typing any piece of work using carbon, it is wise to check that it is not in back to front.

You must take care of carbon paper as it is very temperamental. If it is too hot, the paper will curl - so don't place it near a radiator in the winter! If it is not kept flat it will crease (sometimes known as 'treeing'), and creased carbon paper will show up on your copy. Some carbon papers smudge easily, so take care to have clean fingers.

When you correct the top copy of your work, you must remember to correct the carbon copy as well. If you choose to use correcting fluid, let it dry before continuing to type, otherwise you will find that the correction smears or adheres to the carbon paper itself. If this happens you cannot use that particular piece of carbon paper again.

Remember, your carbon copy should look as neat as your top copy.

WORD DIVISION

In order to keep the right-hand margin as straight as possible, it may be necessary to divide the last word on a line. There are, however, certain rules to follow, and these are given below.

You may divide:

1   Where the word has a 'natural' split
    e.g. tele-phone, demon-strated, mini-mum.
2   At a double consonant
    e.g. get-ting, spel-ling.
3   After a prefix
    e.g. pre-tend, pro-gress, con-fuse.
4   Before a suffix
    e.g. sing-ing, careless-ness.
5   Hyphenated words at the hyphen only
    e.g. part-time, book-keeping.

The hyphen must be on the same line as the first part of the divided word.

You must never divide:

1   A proper name
    e.g. London, Copenhagen, Mr J Armstrong, Dr W Field PhD.
2   A date
    e.g. 22 January 1991, 22/1/91.
3   Time
    e.g. 11.30 am, 1645 hours.
4   Sums of money
    e.g. £86.29, £482,624.81, $23.65

If you are unsure where to divide a word - the rule is **don't**. Press the margin release key so you can finish typing the word, or start the complete word on a new line.

COMMONLY USED ABBREVIATIONS

The following words are commonly abbreviated. They must, however, always be typed in full. It is important to recognise the abbreviated form and be able to spell the full version correctly.

accom	accommodation	misc	miscellaneous
a/c(s)	accounts	necy	necessary
ack	acknowledge	opp(s)	opportunity/ies
advert(s)	advertisement(s)	poss	possible
appt(s)	appointment(s)	p/t	part-time
approx	approximately	rec	receive
beg	begin	recd	received
bel	believe	recom	recommend
bldg(s)	building(s)	ref(s)	reference(s)
bus	business	refd	referred
cat(s)	catalogue(s)	rep(s)	representative(s)
cttee(s)	committee(s)	resp	responsible
co(s)	company/ies	scly/sin	sincerely
def	definitely	sec(s)	secretary/ies
del	delivery	sep	separate
dept	department	sig(s)	signature(s)
dev	develop	suff	sufficient
dr	dear	temp	temporary
enc	enclose	th	that
exp(s)	expense(s)	thro'	through
exp	experience	tog	together
ffly	faithfully	sh	shall
f/t	full-time	shd	should
fwd	forward	w	with
gntee(s)	guarantee(s)	wd	would
gov(s)	government(s)	wh	which
hv	have	wl	will
immed	immediately	y	you
incon	inconvenient/nce	yrs	yours
info	information		
mfr(s)	manufacturer(s)		

The following abbreviations must always be typed in full:

1   Days of the week e.g. Mon - Monday; Wed - Wednesday.
2   Months of the year e.g. Aug - August; Dec - December.
3   Words on addresses e.g. St - Street; Ave - Avenue.
4   Proper names e.g. N York - New York; B'ham - Birmingham.

The following abbreviations can be retained as they are generally accepted:

NB, etc., e.g., Co, Ltd, plc, Inc.
Enc(s) at the end of a letter.
& (ampersand) - when used in company names etc.

TYPES OF HEADINGS

Here is an explanation of the types of headings generally used.

1   THE MAIN HEADING

This is found at the beginning of a piece of work and is usually typed in capital letters. It must always be centred and may be underlined.

2   SUB-HEADING

This is sometimes included as an addition to the information given in the main heading. Turn up 2 lines after the main heading before continuing. This heading is often typed in lower case and may be underlined.

3   SHOULDER HEADING

Shoulder headings are typed in closed capitals at the left-hand margin and can be underlined. After typing this heading, turn up 2 lines before continuing. Shoulder headings are used to separate an article into different main sections.

4   PARAGRAPH HEADINGS

Paragraph headings are always typed in lower case and must be underlined to distinguish them from the rest of the paragraph. They are used to sub-divide an article.

This example shows the various types of heading.

<u>COPY TYPING</u>   (1)

A Guide   (2)

<u>BEFORE STARTING</u>   (3)

Make sure you are sitting comfortably with your feet firmly on the floor. It is important that you have to hand any items of equipment you may require, e.g. a dictionary.

(4)   <u>Spelling mistakes</u> are totally unacceptable, especially when typing proper names. If unsure of the correct spelling of an unfamiliar name do not be embarrassed to ask someone.

Key: (1) = Main heading
         (2) = Sub heading
         (3) = Shoulder heading
         (4) = Paragraph heading

TYPING FIGURES

When typing figures, it is important to make sure that each column lines up correctly as though it were a mathematical sum.

e.g.   1,539
            620
             36
              7

When totalling figures, follow the underlining as shown

e.g.	6,034	212.62	109.25	
	235	1212.26	1212.87	
	72	33.05	654.12	
	8	105.34	1010.65	
	1,241	33.18	434.85	
	132	343.44	354.57	turn up 2 lines
	7,714	2237.89	3777.31	
				turn up 1 line use line spacer

When typing numbered items, if they exceed 9, then the numbers 1–9 will have to be typed **one** space in from the left margin in order to keep the alignment correct.

Use the decimal tab facility.

ROMAN NUMERALS

These may be typed either aligned to the left or aligned to the right, as shown below. It is important to be consistent throughout a piece of work.

Use the small 'i' when typing lower case Roman numerals, and the capital for the upper case ones:

i	vi	XI	XVI
ii	vii	XII	XVII
iii	viii	XIII	XVIII
iv	ix	XIV	XIX
v	x	XV	XX

Chapter 5
Assignments

These assignments are designed to simulate a variety of office situations.

Each assignment consists of several inter-related tasks which consolidate all the skills learnt.

ASSIGNMENT 1   JOB APPLICATION
Task 1   Advertisement
Task 2   Letter
Task 3   Curriculum Vitae
Task 4   Memorandum
Task 5   Interview schedule

ASSIGNMENT 2   TRAVEL AGENCY
Task 1   Holiday offer
Task 2   Letter
Task 3   Itinerary
Task 4   Memo
Task 5   Letter

ASSIGNMENT 3   CATERING COMPANY
Task 1   Letter
Task 2   Sample Menu
Task 3   Memorandum
Task 4   Wine list
Task 5   Letter

ASSIGNMENT 4   HOLIDAY PROPERTY BOOKING
Task 1   Advertisement
Task 2   Letter
Task 3   Checklist
Task 4   Authorisation card
Task 5   General instructions

ASSIGNMENT 5   SALES CONFERENCE
Task 1   Memorandum
Task 2   Hotel information
Task 3   Letter
Task 4   Programme
Task 5   Sales figures

ASSIGNMENT 1   JOB APPLICATION

Task 1

Display this advertisement as if it were to be included in a local newspaper. Make the necessary amendments and correct the circled words.

Printwise Ltd
6 Station Road
Dover
Kent

— Blocked caps

— Centre this section

We are looking for a competetent, enthusiastic Office Junior to assist in our busy Advertising Department.

Duties to include:

General Typing
Answering telephone
Photocopying
Filing

*Inset
10 spaces*

The succesful applicant must be able to type accurately. Training in word proccessing will be given.

For further details and an application form write to: *uc.*

Mrs M Marshall
Personnel Supervisor

Task 2

Type this letter which is in answer to the advertisement in Task 1. Use today's date and type an envelope.

Mrs M Marshall
Personnel Supervisor
Printwise Limited
6 Station Road
Dover
Kent

Dear Mrs Marshall

I am writing with regard to the vacancy for an office junior in the Advertising Department which I saw advertised in our local paper this week.

I should be very glad if you would kindly send me an Application Form and meanwhile I enclose a copy of my Curriculum Vitae for your information.

With many thanks.

Yours sincerely

David White

Enc

Task 3

Prepare this CV for David White on A4 paper which is to be attached to his letter of application.

CURRICULUM VITAE   —   *Centre*

NAME: David White

ADDRESS: 24 Bedford Drive
                 Dover
                 Kent
TELEPHONE: 0634 2998

DATE OF BIRTH: 18 March 1974

EDUCATION AND QUALIFICATIONS

Sept 1985-90   Dover Comprehensive School
                    Qualifications
                    GCSE - English   ~~B~~ **A**
                           Maths   B
                           History   C
                           Geography B
                           CDT   A

                    Captain of Rugby team
                    Member of school orchestra (clarinet)

WORK EXPERIENCE

May 1990   Three weeks Work Experience with:

                         Radley Thomas Limited: Duties
                         included typing, filing, basic office work.

                         I have also done odd jobs for neighbours
                         such as: baby-sitting, car-washing
                         etc.

HOBBIES

I enjoy listening to music and reading. I play for a local
rugby team and I swim for charity.

I have just passed my driving test.

OTHER INFORMATION

I can type at 30 words per minute. I am a member of the local
youth club and have organised several trips for up to 25
members at a time.

Task 4

Prepare this memo to John Walker, correcting where indicated.

To: John Walker
Advertising Manager

From: Maureen Marshall
Personnel Supervisor

Date:

Subject: Office Junior —— Caps and us

We have had a very good response to our advertisement for the above position within your Dept.

I enclose a schedule for the interviews wh are to take place next Tues in uc rooms 103/108.

Please let me know if you wish to alter any of the times.

Task 5

Prepare this interview schedule.

INTERVIEWS — OFFICE JUNIOR } (centre)
Advertising Department

Name	Room	Time
Helena Price	103	9.45
Michael Ward	103	10.30
COFFEE		
David White	108	11.45
Shona Patel	108	12.30
LUNCH		
Melissa Smith-Thomas	108	2.30
Jennifer Charalanbous	103	3.15

Typist — Double line spacing throughout please

ASSIGNMENT 2　TRAVEL AGENCY

Task 1

Prepare the following which is to be displayed in the travel agent's window.

THE CITY TRAVEL AGENTS — sp. caps and u/s

SPECIAL OFFERS — AUGUST — u/s
VISIT PARIS; ROME OR BRUSSELS

SPEND 10 DAYS IN A LUXURY HOTEL ⎫ single
IN THE CENTRE OF ONE OF THE　　⎬ line
ABOVE CITIES　　　　　　　　　　⎭ spacing

DAYTIME FLIGHTS FROM HEATHROW — u/s

Further information contact:
Debbie Mills — "Specials Desk."

Task 2

Prepare this letter which refers to the Special Offer holiday.

Mr & Mrs Clarke
Lmks Cottage
Peartree Road
Windsor
WS4 6PR

Dear Mr & Mrs C——

Thank you for the interest you have
uc shown in our "Special offer" holiday
and for your deposit of £70.00.

I can now confirm your holiday booking
⟨✓⟩ to France [Paris] in Aug. You will be staying
at the Hotel Splendide for 9 nights /
10 days.

run
on The hotel is situated only a few minutes
walk from the Eiffel Tower.

Enclosed are the flight details which
are subject to change at short notice.
We will send you [an invoice for] the final balance
approx 6 weeks before your departure
date. ←

yrs scly

Debbie Mills

Your tickets will be sent
2 weeks before your
holiday.

Task 3

This itinerary/information is to be sent with the letter to Mr and Mrs Clarke.

ITINERARY

Typist - please add abbreviation hrs after all times

12 August 19..
Flight no AF 145

stet   Depart ~~London Heathrow~~ 10.45   Arrive Paris 11.50
                    Heathrow   Charles de Gaulle

Transfer to Hotel Splendide using hotel's courtesy bus.

9 nights at Hotel Splendide - half board

22 August 19..
Flight no AF 146

Depart Paris 14.30   Arrive London 1515
       Charles de Gaulle   Heathrow

NB — All times - local time.

Task 4

Prepare this memo on A5 paper. The subject is: Flight Time Change.

From : Air France
To: All Travel Agents

The time of flight AF145 to Paris during Aug has been changed. The flight now departs one hour earlier at 9.45am, arriving in Paris at 1050.

Please inform all your clients of this alteration.

run on We apologies for any incon this may cause.

Typist - use 24-hour clock on <u>all</u> times

Task 5

Prepare this letter to Mr and Mrs Clarke.

On a piece of A6 paper (half of A5), type the name and address of Mr and Mrs Clarke, in capital letters throughout, to represent a label which could be used on a large envelope.

Dear Mr & Mrs C _____

insert/ Ⓐ NP We have pleasure in enclosing the tickets ∧ for your forthcoming holiday. || Please note the earlier departure time of your outward flight, as mentioned during our telephone conversation of last week. || NP We confirm that ∧ non you will be on a ∧ smoking flight & that your seat numbers are E41 & E42.

We hope you have an enjoyable trip.

Yours sincerely

Debbie Mills

Ⓐ and luggage labels

ASSIGNMENT 3   CATERING COMPANY

Task 1

Prepare the following letter to Mr and Mrs J Aldridge of 79 The Cricket Green, Norwich, Norfolk.

Dear Mr & Mrs A_____

Many thanks for yr letter of the 8th Feb.
uc   we shall be pleased to supply you with everything you require for yr daughter's
uc   wedding on 24th July.

Arranging weddings can be very worrying and it is our policy to take away the pressure & ensure that all goes smoothly — as far as the catering is concerned.

We enclose a Brochure & price lists which
cold\ range from £4.60 per head for a \ buffet, to £17.50 per head for a sit down meal. [When
NP   you have had a chance to look at our Brochure and price lists, perhaps you
uc   would like to contact Miss Sue Lordell who will be co-ordinating all the arrangements for your daughter's wedding.

Yrs scly

JAMESON CATERERS PLC

Peter Jameson
Managing Director

Enc

Task 2

Prepare this sample menu, centring both horizontally and vertically.

Jameson Caterers plc — u/s

SAMPLE MENU —   Spaced Cap
£4.60 per head

Chicken Coronation

Salmon Puffs

Mushroom/ Ham Vol au Vents

Green Salad
Rice Salad
Potato   "
Pasta   "

Raspberry Fool
Lemon Pudding

Coffee

Typist —
Don't use ditto marks.

Task 3

Prepare this memo from Peter Jameson to Sue Lordell. The subject heading is: Wedding – Mr and Mrs Aldridge.

You will see from the enclosed copies of correspondence received from the above, & my reply, that I have assigned this particular job to you.

It might be an idea to either telephone the Aldridges or call on them personally to give them any help assistance they might need in these initial stages.

Encs

Task 4

Display the following, ruling up as shown.

JAMESON CATERERS plc — u/s

Suggested Wedding Wine List — CAPS

Cost per Glass	£0.75	£0.90	£1.20	£1.50
On arrival	Fruit juice	Sherry	—	—
First course	—	White wine	—	—
Main "	Rosé	" "	Red wine	—
Dessert "	—	" "	" "	—
Coffee	—	—	—	Liqueurs

uc (On arrival)
uc (First course)

Champagne @ £1.60 per glass to be served for the "Toast".

Typist — No ditto marks.

Task 5

Prepare this letter to Jameson Caterers from Mr Aldridge.

Miss S Lovdell

J—— C —— plc

White Towers

St Henry's Walk

NORWICH

Norfolk

Dear Miss L ———

We felt we had to write to say thank you for the wonderful way in which you handled all the catering arrangements for our daughter's wedding wh took

∧ last | place ∧ Saturday.

The whole day went so smoothly we were

NP all able to enjoy it to the full. // We recd numerous compliments on the presentation and quality of the food. One of our friends will, in fact, be contacting you in the near future with regard

u.c to a _ruby_ _wedding_ party.

Many thanks again for your splendid service.

yours scly

John Aldridge

ASSIGNMENT 4   HOLIDAY PROPERTY BOOKING

Task 1

Display the following advertisement for entry in a holiday brochure.

<u>CORNWALL</u>

Delightful Period Cottage to let;

4 Bedrooms, 2 Receptions, Kitchen.

Beautiful south facing garden overlooking safe beach.

Ideally situated, close to local shops.

Leisure centre 1 mile;

m/ Accompdation will suit 4 adults and up to 6 children; Cot available on request.

1 or 2 week lets available during summer.

Contact:

trs Mrs Drinkwater - 01632 - 49783

Smugglers Cottage
Plunder Lane
Little Cove
St Ives
Cornwall

Task 2

Prepare this letter to Mrs Drinkwater (address shown on advertisement):

Today's date

Dear Mrs D_____

Further to our telephone conversation, I have pleasure in enclosing our deposit of £20 for a 2 week holiday covering the dates 6th to 20th July inclusive.

We understand we are fully resp for the cottage and that we have to provide our own linen & towels. [As agreed, we wl collect the key from the Post office in the village as near to 4.00pm on the 6th as poss. We look forward to receiving the card authorising us to do this.

Many thanks for all your help.

Yrs scly

Claire Goddard

Enc

Task 3

Tabulate the following. Use appropriate-sized paper.

Holiday checklist — caps & u/s

Food	Linen	std Medical Medicines	Clothes
Milk	Towels	Aspirin	Swimsuit
Bread	Sheets	Bandages	Shorts
Butter	Pillow cases	Plasters	T-shirts
lc Jam	Beach Bag	Cream	Jeans
Bacon	Flannel	Safety pins	Dress
Eggs	Tea towels	Scissors	Sweatshirts

Task 4

Prepare this authorisation card and fill in the appropriate details.

| This confirms that Mr/Mrs.................... have booked SMUGGLERS COTTAGE from....................... to.......................

 Please hand them the key. | SMUGGLERS COTTAGE
 PLUNDER LANE
 LITTLE COVE
 ST IVES
 CORNWALL |

Typist: This section in double line spacing

Task 5

Re-key this checklist making the necessary corrections.

SMUGGLERS COTTAGE

General instructions

lc 1   On Arrival, switch on Gas and Electricity located in cupboard above kitchen sink.

3   Before lighting a fire, check grate is clear of ashes - replenish logs on departure.

2   Meters take 50p coins only.

4   Do not hang washing infront garden, there is a rotating dryer in broom cupboard for back garden use.

5   The local shop will deliver milk daily on request.

uc 6   The butcher is open every day except thursday and Sunday.

7   The bakery bakes fresh bread every day including Sundays - the croissants for breakfast are a 'must'.

8   Information on local attractions is displayed outside the Post Office. They will also take bookings for any of the outings shown on the hall desk - please give 2 days notice.

9   In case of emergency:

Doctor - Dr John Evans - Tel No. 46728
Dentist - Andrew Pegram - Tel No. 43865

am 10   Please leave cottage clean and tidy at 11.00 on the day of departure and return keys to the Post Office.

Typist - Keep layout as shown. Note changed order.

ASSIGNMENT 5   SALES CONFERENCE

Task 1

Prepare this memorandum from the Conference Co-ordinator to the Sales Director.

Subject – Annual Sales Conference

Attached are the details of the new venue for the forthcoming Sales

uc   <u>c</u>onference.

This Hotel has been selected as they are able to offer a wide range of facilities which were sadly lacking at last year's

NP   conference. [You will see from my letter that we have reserved the Windsor Room which will suit our needs.

Task 2

Display effectively this hotel leaflet which is to be sent with the memo in task 1.

THREE LAWNS HOTEL — spaced Caps and Centre

are pleased to announce the opening of their newly furbished Conference Rooms

Facilities available include:

Qualified Secretarial Staff
Word Processing facilities
Electronic mailbox
Facsimile machines
Photocopying
OHP and Whiteboard
Telephone points

Catering:

Tea and coffee available throughout the day

Buffet Luncheon (on request)

Conference Rooms:

Windsor — Up to 50 people
Sandringham — " " 150 "
Caernarfon — " " 250 "

Contact:

Alison Roberts — Assistant Manager
Ext 209

Task 3

Prepare this letter, take a copy and type an envelope.

Miss A Roberts
Assistant Manager
Three Lawns Hotel
Harrogate
Yorks
YK5 1HA

Dear Miss Roberts

I wd like to book 9 single rooms
with private bath/shower for the night
NP   of 14th July. [I also confirm the telephone
⊘   booking of the ~~Sandringham~~ Windsor Conference
Room for the 15th July. The facilities
we require are:

Inset   ⌈Facsimile machine
6 spaces |OHP and whiteboard
            |Secretarial Services
            ⌊Buffet lunch for 30 people

As also mentioned there will be 7
↑the people for a private dinner on/evening
of the 14th, I understand this will
be served in your Berkeley Room.

Yours scly

R Palmer
Conference Coordinator

Task 4

Set out the following programme. Keep all times to the 24-hour clock.

Annual Sales Conference *(caps / underscore)*
15th July 19..

Time			Personnel
0900	Meet for Coffee		
0930	Welcome / Introduction		Roger Palmer
9.45	Area Reports from Managers:	Scotland	Ian Mackintosh
		Midlands	Louise Bullivant
		London-N	Roger Patel
		London-S	Winston Cosby
1115	Coffee *(caps)*		
1130	Area Reports (continued)		
		Home Counties	Simon Charles
		West Country	Rita Simmons
1300	Lunch *(caps)*		
1400	Presentations		Neville Day Sales Manager
2.30	New Directions		Guest Speaker
3.30	Tea *(caps)*		
1545	Farewell		

Typist — Double line spacing between times.

Task 5

Display the sales figures shown below. No ruling required.

Sales Figures — CAPS & U|S

Area	1990	1991	Estimated Forecast	
Scotland	12,589	15,671	18,300	⎫
Midlands	17,636	20,483	23,000	⎬ Double
London - North	22,785	24,291	26,000	line
" - South	21,639	23,638	25,500	spacing.
Home Counties	15,391	19,891	22,000	
West Country	13,486	12,912*	15,000	⎭

* Drop in sales figures due to long-term illness of local rep who has since retired.

Index